DAVID O. MCKAY LIBRARY

P9-DVD-838

AUG 0 6 2014

WITHDRAWN

JUN 1 8 2024

DAVID O. McKAY LIBRARY
BYU-IDAHO

PROPERTY OF:
DAVID O. McKAY LIBRARY
BYU-IDAHO
REXBURG ID 83460-0405

INTRODUCING
ISSUES WITH
OPPOSING
VIEWPOINTS®

Juvenile Crime

Jacqueline Langwith, *Book Editor*

GREENHAVEN PRESS
A part of Gale, Cengage Learning

GALE
CENGAGE Learning·

Farmington Hills, Mich • San Francisco • New York • Waterville, Maine
Meriden, Conn • Mason, Ohio • Chicago

Elizabeth Des Chenes, *Director, Content Strategy*
Cynthia Sanner, *Publisher*
Douglas Dentino, *Manager, New Product*

© 2014 Greenhaven Press, a part of Gale, Cengage Learning

WCN: 01-100-101

Gale and Greenhaven Press are registered trademarks used herein under license.

For more information, contact:
Greenhaven Press
27500 Drake Rd.
Farmington Hills, MI 48331-3535
Or you can visit our Internet site at gale.cengage.com

ALL RIGHTS RESERVED.
No part of this work covered by the copyright herein may be reproduced, transmitted, stored, or used in any form or by any means graphic, electronic, or mechanical, including but not limited to photocopying, recording, scanning, digitizing, taping, Web distribution, information networks, or information storage and retrieval systems, except as permitted under Section 107 or 108 of the 1976 United States Copyright Act, without the prior written permission of the publisher.

For product information and technology assistance, contact us at

Gale Customer Support, 1-800-877-4253
For permission to use material from this text or product, submit all requests online at
www.cengage.com/permissions

Further permissions questions can be e-mailed to permissionrequest@cengage.com

Articles in Greenhaven Press anthologies are often edited for length to meet page requirements. In addition, original titles of these works are changed to clearly present the main thesis and to explicitly indicate the author's opinion. Every effort is made to ensure that Greenhaven Press accurately reflects the original intent of the authors. Every effort has been made to trace the owners of copyrighted material.

Cover image © Fisun Ivan/Shutterstock.com.

LIBRARY OF CONGRESS CATALOGING-IN-PUBLICATION DATA

Juvenile crime / Jacqueline Langwith, book editor.
    pages cm. -- (Introducing issues with opposing viewpoints)
  Summary: "IIOVP: Juvenile Crime: This title explores the causes of juvenile crime, how the justice system should treat juvenile offenders, and how juvenile crime can be reduced"-- Provided by publisher.
  Includes bibliographical references and index.
  Audience: Grade 9-12.
  ISBN 978-0-7377-6925-8 (hardback)
  1. Juvenile delinquency--United States--Juvenile literature. 2. Juvenile delinquents--United States--Juvenile literature. 3. Juvenile justice, Administration of--United States--Juvenile literature. 4. Juvenile corrections--United States--Juvenile literature. I. Langwith, Jacqueline.
  HV9104.J83192 2014
  364.360973--dc23
                                       2014002819

Printed in the United States of America
1 2 3 4 5 6 7 18 17 16 15 14

Contents

Chapter 3: How Can Juvenile Crime Be Reduced?

Foreword

Indulging in a wide spectrum of ideas, beliefs, and perspectives is a critical cornerstone of democracy. After all, it is often debates over differences of opinion, such as whether to legalize abortion, how to treat prisoners, or when to enact the death penalty, that shape our society and drive it forward. Such diversity of thought is frequently regarded as the hallmark of a healthy and civilized culture. As the Reverend Clifford Schutjer of the First Congregational Church in Mansfield, Ohio, declared in a 2001 sermon, "Surrounding oneself with only like-minded people, restricting what we listen to or read only to what we find agreeable is irresponsible. Refusing to entertain doubts once we make up our minds is a subtle but deadly form of arrogance." With this advice in mind, Introducing Issues with Opposing Viewpoints books aim to open readers' minds to the critically divergent views that comprise our world's most important debates.

Introducing Issues with Opposing Viewpoints simplifies for students the enormous and often overwhelming mass of material now available via print and electronic media. Collected in every volume is an array of opinions that captures the essence of a particular controversy or topic. Introducing Issues with Opposing Viewpoints books embody the spirit of nineteenth-century journalist Charles A. Dana's axiom: "Fight for your opinions, but do not believe that they contain the whole truth, or the only truth." Absorbing such contrasting opinions teaches students to analyze the strength of an argument and compare it to its opposition. From this process readers can inform and strengthen their own opinions, or be exposed to new information that will change their minds. Introducing Issues with Opposing Viewpoints is a mosaic of different voices. The authors are statesmen, pundits, academics, journalists, corporations, and ordinary people who have felt compelled to share their experiences and ideas in a public forum. Their words have been collected from newspapers, journals, books, speeches, interviews, and the Internet, the fastest growing body of opinionated material in the world.

Introducing Issues with Opposing Viewpoints shares many of the well-known features of its critically acclaimed parent series, Opposing Viewpoints. The articles are presented in a pro/con format, allowing readers to absorb divergent perspectives side by side. Active reading questions preface each viewpoint, requiring the student to approach the material thoughtfully and carefully. Useful charts, graphs, and cartoons supplement each article. A thorough introduction provides readers with crucial background on an issue. An annotated bibliography points the reader toward articles, books, and websites that contain additional information on the topic. An appendix of organizations to contact contains a wide variety of charities, nonprofit organizations, political groups, and private enterprises that each hold a position on the issue at hand. Finally, a comprehensive index allows readers to locate content quickly and efficiently.

Introducing Issues with Opposing Viewpoints is also significantly different from Opposing Viewpoints. As the series title implies, its presentation will help introduce students to the concept of opposing viewpoints and learn to use this material to aid in critical writing and debate. The series' four-color, accessible format makes the books attractive and inviting to readers of all levels. In addition, each viewpoint has been carefully edited to maximize a reader's understanding of the content. Short but thorough viewpoints capture the essence of an argument. A substantial, thought-provoking essay question placed at the end of each viewpoint asks the student to further investigate the issues raised in the viewpoint, compare and contrast two authors' arguments, or consider how one might go about forming an opinion on the topic at hand. Each viewpoint contains sidebars that include at-a-glance information and handy statistics. A Facts About section located in the back of the book further supplies students with relevant facts and figures.

Following in the tradition of the Opposing Viewpoints series, Greenhaven Press continues to provide readers with invaluable exposure to the controversial issues that shape our world. As John Stuart Mill once wrote: "The only way in which a human being can make some approach to knowing the whole of a subject is by hearing what can be said about it by persons of every variety of opinion and studying all modes in which it can be looked at by every character of mind. No wise man ever acquired his wisdom in any mode but this." It is to this principle that Introducing Issues with Opposing Viewpoints books are dedicated.

Introduction

Violence interrupters are asked to go into the most dangerous neighborhoods, in the most dangerous cities in the U.S., at the most dangerous times, to get people to stop shooting each other. And they're going in unarmed. Yet, they go in, and they do it. And it works. It's really changed my view about what's possible.

—Daniel Webster, deputy director of Johns Hopkins Center for the Prevention of Youth Violence

The 2011 documentary film *The Interrupters* chronicles three people trying to stop—or interrupt—the spread of violence on the South Side of Chicago, in Illiniois in 2009. The trailer for the film begins with one of the "interrupters," an African American woman named Ameena, speaking at the funeral of a young victim of violent crime. The next scene shows teddy bears and balloons surrounding a car and a tree—makeshift shrines to two other young persons slain in Chicago that year. After several more scenes showing police tape and screaming ambulances, the following words gradually appear on the screen: "VIOLENCE is like a DISEASE . . . it SPREADS from ONE PERSON to ANOTHER . . . to CURE IT you need to INTERRUPT IT."[1] *The Interrupters* film depicts an approach to violence prevention that is based on the idea that violence is a contagious disease and stopping its spread requires treating "the infection" at its source.

The notion that violence is a contagious disease is based on its having certain characteristics that are similar to infectious diseases. According to social scientists who champion this concept, exposure to violence is similar to being exposed to an infectious pathogen like cholera, smallpox, or the influenza virus. While exposure to these diseases occurs by breathing in, touching, or ingesting the disease-causing microorganism, exposure to violence occurs when people witness or are victimized by it. Scientists say that something happens in the brains of these people that makes them more likely to carry out violence on others, and the scientists liken this to being "infected" with violence. Once people are infected, they are more likely to perpetuate violence against others. This creates more victims and witnesses and is how violence spreads.

Speaking at the Forum on Global Violence Prevention hosted by the Institute of Medicine in 2011, University of Michigan psychology professor L. Rowell Huesmann explained the contagion of violence. "Violent communities and neighborhoods breed violence in those who join the community or neighborhood," he said. "Introducing violence into a community increases the risk of greater violence throughout the community. It even appears to be true within nations and cultures. And it is true across generations. Children catch it from their parents, and parents can catch it from their children."[2]

Understanding the infectious nature of violence is essential to preventing it, say social scientists. They contend that society's attempts to address violence by imprisonment have not been effective, because punishment is not the way to address an infectious disease. According to epidemiologist Gary Slutkin, a founder of the Chicago violence interrupters program, before the discovery that bacteria and viruses caused diseases, society labeled persons who came down with smallpox, cholera, or other diseases as morally corrupt, or "bad." In a paper presented at a 2013 workshop on the contagion of violence, Slutkin writes, "The problem of violence, like the great infectious diseases of the past, has been stuck—not because we do not care enough, nor because we do not have enough money devoted to it, but because we have made the wrong diagnosis. Wrong diagnoses, in particular moralistic diagnoses, usually lead to ineffective and even counterproductive treatments and control strategies."[3]

In an interview with the Robert Wood Johnson Foundation in 2011, Slutkin compares violence to tuberculosis (TB) to illustrate how violence can be prevented by using the understanding that it is an infectious disease:

> You have someone who's coughing a lot and has TB and is spreading it to his friends and family. He needs to be put on anti-tuberculosis therapy to prevent that spread as well as for the cure of himself.
>
> Now, take someone who is about to shoot somebody. This person has to be prevented from spreading more of this and so he needs

to be persuaded from doing what he was thinking of because that will cause more and more events [of violence].

Then think about the TB patient. You've cooled his disease process down, but then if you don't keep working with him over the course of the next few months it will reemerge. So you have to keep working with him for six months or a year with anti-tuberculosis therapy. These high-risk individuals, although they may have been persuaded out of one or two events, you now have to keep working with them to change their thinking so that they will not [engage in violence] the next time that they are motivated to or provoked or riled up.[4]

Since prisons and juvenile detention centers tend to be very violent places, incarceration can facilitate the spread of violence, rather than stop it, say scientists. Male and female prisoners are frequently assaulted by other prisoners and even by guards. The nonprofit Annie E. Casey Foundation has found that teens in juvenile facilities across the country also face violence and abuse.

According to Barry Krisberg, a professor from the University of California–Berkeley, there is good reason to assume that sources of violence spread violence among prisoners, family members, the children of prisoners, and in the communities where released inmates return. However, Krisberg says more research on this topic is needed. What is clear, according to Krisberg, is that the use of imprisonment as the first response to violence should be reevaluated because history has shown that responding to public health issues such as tuberculosis, polio, mental illness, and HIV with the incapacitation and isolation of affected individuals has not been very effective.

Some people, particularly gun rights supporters, oppose calling violence—especially gun violence—a disease. Chuck Grassley, a US senator from Iowa, spoke against President Barack Obama's directive to the Centers for Disease Control and Prevention to conduct research into the causes of gun violence. Said Grassley,

Gun violence is not a disease, and lawful gun ownership is not a disease. It is a constitutionally protected individual right, the famous Second Amendment right, not only part of the Constitution for 225 years but reinforced by two recent Supreme

Court decisions. The president said that we suffer from an—quote, 'epidemic of violence,' end of quote. Although there is too much violence in America, violent crime rates are at the lowest level in 50 years, not at epidemic levels, at least epidemic when compared to the—prior to the last 50 years.[5]

While Grassley does not think gun violence is a disease, scientists like Huesmann, Slutkin, and Krisberg think that viewing all violence—including gun violence—as a disease is the best way to prevent it. They think that viewing disease as a public health issue may help prevent the deaths of some young people, unlike the young boy in the coffin at the funeral where Ameena spoke.

In *Introducing Issues with Opposing Viewpoints: Juvenile Crime*, the authors provide their perspectives on the causes of juvenile crime and violence, how the criminal justice system should treat juvenile offenders, and how juvenile crime can be reduced.

Notes

1. *The Interrupters*, directed by Steve James. Chicago: Kartemquin Films, 2011. http://cureviolence.org/the-interrupters.
2. L. Rowell Huesmann, "The Contagion of Violence: The Extent, the Processes, and the Outcomes," address delivered at the National Academies of Sciences' Institute of Medicine's Forum on Global Violence Prevention, Washington, DC, April 29, 2011.
3. Gary Slutkin, *Violence Is a Contagious Disease*. Washington, DC: National Academies, 2013.
4. Quoted in NewPublicHealth, Robert Wood Johnson Foundation, "*The Interrupters*: A NewPublicHealth Q&A with Gary Slutkin," September 29, 2011. www.rwjf.org/en/blogs/new-public -health/2011/09/the-interrupters-a-newpublichealth-qa-with-gary -slutkin.html.
5. Quoted in Eleanor Taylor-Nicholson, and Barry Krisberg, *Contagion of Violence*. Washington, DC: National Academies, 2013.

Chapter 1

What Are the Causes of Juvenile Crime and Violence?

Juvenile crime is caused by a number of social and economic factors.

Violent Video Games Contribute to Juvenile Violence

Iowa State University News Service

"Both the frequency of play and affinity for violent games were strongly associated with delinquent and violent behavior."

In the following viewpoint Iowa State University researchers contend that exposure to violent video games is strongly linked to juvenile violence and delinquency. The researchers analyzed video game exposure and violence among youth in Pennsylvania. They found that youth who frequently play violent video games were more likely to have exhibited violent and delinquent behavior, even after controlling for many other factors. The Iowa State University News Service reports on the major research findings of faculty and scientists at the school.

AS YOU READ, CONSIDER THE FOLLOWING QUESTIONS:

1. What was the average number of violent acts committed by the Pennsylvania youth in the Iowa State University study, as stated in the viewpoint?
2. What is the cutting edge of research into studying serious aggression, according to Douglas Gentile in the viewpoint?
3. According to Matt DeLisi, as quoted by the author, for what type of child would it be unhealthy to be allowed to escape inside him- or herself for a long period?

"Violent Video Games Are a Risk Factor for Criminal Behavior and Aggression," http:news.iastate.edu, March 25, 2013. Copyright © 2013 by Iowa State University News Service. All rights reserved. Reproduced with permission.

People are quick to point the finger or dismiss the effect of violent video games as a factor in criminal behavior. New evidence from Iowa State researchers demonstrates a link between video games and youth violence and delinquency.

Matt DeLisi, a professor of sociology, said the research shows a strong connection even when controlling for a history of violence and psychopathic traits among juvenile offenders.

"When critics say, 'Well, it's probably not video games, it's probably how antisocial they are,' we can address that directly because we controlled for a lot of things that we know matter," DeLisi said. "Even if you account for the child's sex, age, race, the age they were first referred to juvenile court—which is a very powerful effect—and a bunch of other media effects, like screen time and exposure. Even with all of that, the video game measure still mattered."

The author analyzed video game exposure and violence among youth in Pennsylvania and found that youth who frequently play violent video games are more likely to exhibit violent and delinquent behavior.

Video Game Exposure Is a Strong Risk Factor, but Not the Only One

The results were not unexpected, but somewhat surprising for Douglas Gentile, an associate professor of psychology, who has studied the effects of video game violence exposure and minor aggression, like hitting, teasing and name-calling.

"I didn't expect to see much of an effect when we got to serious delinquent and criminal level aggression because youth who commit that level of aggression have a lot of things going wrong for them. They often have a lot of risk factors and very few protective factors in their lives," Gentile said.

The study published in the April [2013] issue of *Youth Violence and Juvenile Justice* examined the level of video game exposure for 227 juvenile offenders in Pennsylvania. The average offender had committed nearly nine serious acts of violence, such as gang fighting, hitting a parent or attacking another person in the prior year.

The results show that both the frequency of play and affinity for violent games were strongly associated with delinquent and violent behavior. Craig Anderson, Distinguished Professor of psychology and director of the Center for the Study of Violence at Iowa State, said violent video game exposure is not the sole cause of violence, but this study shows it is a risk factor.

FAST FACT

Death Race, released in 1976, is noted as the first violent video game in the United States.

"Can we say from this study that Adam Lanza [the twenty-year-old who killed twenty students and six adults at Sandy Hook Elementary School in Connecticut, along with his mother and himself, in December 2012], or any of the others, went off and killed people because of media violence? You can't take the stand of the NRA [National Rifle Association] that it's strictly video games and not guns," Anderson said. "You also can't take the stand of the entertainment industry that it has nothing to do with media violence, that it's all about guns and not about media violence. They're both wrong and they're both right, both are causal risk factors."

Researchers point out that juvenile offenders have several risk factors that influence their behavior. The next step is to build on this

Most People Believe There Is a Link Between Video-Game Playing and Teen Violence

Percent who agree video games can influence teens' violent behavior

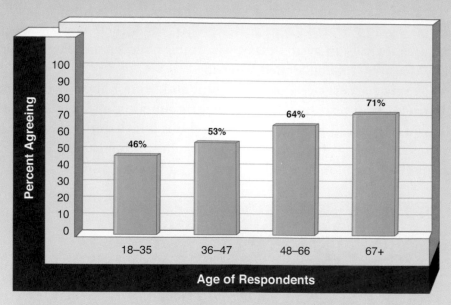

Taken from: Survey of 2,278 adults interviewed online by Harris Poll in January 2013.

research to determine what combination of factors is the most volatile and if there is a saturation point.

"When studying serious aggression, looking at multiple risk factors matters more than looking at any one," Gentile said. "The cutting edge of research is trying to understand in what combination do the individual risk factors start influencing each other in ways to either enhance or mitigate the odds of aggression?"

Message for Parents

There is a lot of misinformation about video game exposure, Anderson said, that makes it difficult for parents to understand the harmful effects. Although it is one variable that parents can control, he understands that with mixed messages about the risks some parents may feel it's not worth the effort.

"What parent would go through the pain and all the effort it takes to really control their child's media diet, if they don't really think it makes any difference? That is why it is so important to get out the simple and clear message that media violence does matter," Anderson said.

Just because a child plays a violent video game does not mean he or she is going to act violently. Researchers say if there is a take away for parents, it is an awareness of what their children are playing and how that may influence their behavior.

"I think parents need to be truthful and honest about who their children are in terms of their psychiatric functioning," DeLisi said. "If you have a kid who is antisocial, who is a little bit vulnerable to influence, giving them something that allows them to escape into themselves for a long period of time isn't a healthy thing."

EVALUATING THE AUTHOR'S ARGUMENTS:

Did this viewpoint convince you that exposure to violent video games is linked to youth violence? If so, why? If not, what type of information, if added to the viewpoint, would have made it more likely that you would have been convinced?

Viewpoint

2

Violent Video Games Have Not Been Proven to Contribute to Juvenile Violence

Christopher J. Ferguson

"I find no evidence that video games or television contribute to youth violence, dating violence, bullying, or adult arrests."

In the following viewpoint Christopher J. Ferguson, an associate professor of psychology at Texas A&M University, asserts that there is no evidence linking video games to youth violence. Ferguson, who is interested in the causes of violent behavior, questions the belief that video games contribute to youth violence. He contends that in his research he found no evidence linking video games to violent behavior. According to Ferguson, when national tragedies such as the 2012 Sandy Hook Elementary School shooting occur, in which a twenty-year-old shooter killed twenty students, six adults, his mother, and himself, many scholars, driven by emotion, make unsupported claims about video games' link to violence.

Christopher J. Ferguson, "Don't Blame Video Games for Real-World Violence," *The Chronicle of Higher Education,* January 10, 2012. Reproduced with permission.

AS YOU READ, CONSIDER THE FOLLOWING QUESTIONS:
1. Did the person responsible for the Virginia Tech shooting play violent video games, according to Ferguson?
2. According to the author, two scholars incorrectly believed that video games likely contributed to the Sandy Hook Elementary School shooting. Who are these two scholars?
3. What has happened to the levels of youth violence since the video game epoch, according to Ferguson?

After the 2007 Virginia Tech shooting, pundits such as TV's Dr. Phil and politicians like Mitt Romney stated emphatically that video games were one cause of the tragedy. Later, in the official investigation, it emerged that the shooter did not play violent games. This rather embarrassing lesson should serve as a warning about rushing to judgment and the need to remain cautious in making causal attributions in the wake of national tragedies. In the case of Virginia Tech, the scientific community generally remained responsible in not rushing to claim links between video games and the shooting.

Killing of Innocents Causes Emotional but Unfounded Claims Against Video Games

Not so after the awful Sandy Hook [Elementary School] event this past December [2012]. Granted, the murder of so many innocents [twenty students and six adults at the school were killed, along with the shooter, Adam Lanza, and his mother] is a grueling national horror like few others, and such events naturally cause people to act emotionally. But even though we know little yet about Adam Lanza's media use, and despite an absence of research linking video-game violence to societal violence or mass shootings, a number of scholars have drawn direct links between video games and the Sandy Hook event specifically.

One prominent scholar, Craig Anderson, at Iowa State University, told a reporter that video games probably contributed to the Sandy Hook shooting. Another scholar, Kirstie Farrar, at the University of Connecticut, claimed that "there's no debate in the academic community" about the positive correlation between video games and aggression, in a news article in which, ironically, I and other scholars debated her position. She was also quoted as saying that video games may be contributing to the increase in mass shootings in recent years, despite no evidence for that claim and the fact shootings have been holding steady, not increasing, according to that criminologist James Alan Fox.

In the past, scholars have been careful to note that research on aggression—like having college students fill in the missing letters of word (such that filling in a word as "explode" as opposed to "explore" would be considered more aggressive)—could not easily be generalized to societal violence. But among many scholars, such caution has been dropped in the wake of Sandy Hook.

To be sure, some scholars continue to be voices of reason. Frank Farley, former American Psychological Association (APA) president, reminds us in a piece in *Psychology Today* that social science has little to offer on questions of societal violence. And the APA itself has generally been cautious thus far in its approach to Sandy Hook. But some scholars risk damaging not only their own credibility but that of the scientific field by making hyperbolic and sometimes blatantly misleading statements the data can't support.

Research Is Inconsistent

First, a quick review of the statistics. There exists a pool of several hundred studies on media violence. These studies have always been inconsistent, despite some unfortunate claims by some scholars to the contrary. Recent reviews of this research, ranging from the 2001 Department of Health and Human Services report on youth violence through recent reviews of video-game research by the U.S. Supreme Court and the governments of Australia and Sweden, have all concluded that the research is inconsistent and weakened by methodological flaws.

FAST FACT

According to the Entertainment Software Ratings Board, 97 percent of parents report always or sometimes monitoring the games their children play.

It's true the American Academy of Pediatrics has claimed that media violence is a cause of societal violence, but its policy statements have been found to be riddled with errors, like inflating something

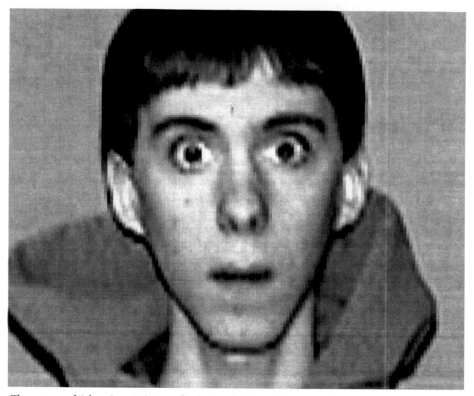

The actions of Adam Lanza (pictured), the Sandy Hook Elementary shooter, stirred up accusations against video game violence that were emotionally based but unfounded, argues the author.

as simple as the number of studies by a factor of 10 and repeating discredited scientific urban legends such as that the effects of media violence are similar to secondhand smoking on lung cancer (something that should never have survived the "sniff test").

Few studies actually examine violent behavior as outcomes, and those that do are least likely to find evidence for negative effects. In my own research, I find no evidence that video games or television contribute to youth violence, dating violence, bullying, or adult arrests. Further, the societal-violence data don't support the effects hypothesis. Youth violence has declined to 40-year lows during the video-game epoch, and countries that consume as much violent media as we do, such as Canada, the Netherlands, and South Korea, have much less violent crime, even if you factor out gun violence. Some scholars try to claim that societal data are irrelevant, but when they link media use to national tragedies they themselves open the door to look at the societal data.

Video Games Are Not a Common Thread

Lastly, violent-media consumption is not a commonality among mass-homicide perpetrators. We focus, irrationally, on it in cases where the perpetrator is a young male like Adam Lanza, since almost all young males consume violent media. But when the perpetrator is an older male, such as 62-year-old William Spengler, who killed two volunteer firefighters the week after Sandy Hook, or the rare woman, such as Amy Bishop, the 44-year-old biology professor who killed three at her university in 2010, video games simply aren't mentioned. This kind of confirmation bias allows us to think video games are a common thread when they are not.

I do understand that scholars are sincerely reacting to an emotional event. But I call upon them to be much more careful, cautious, and responsible in their public statements. Claiming there is consistent research linking video games with aggression and certainly with mass shootings cannot be supported by the available data. Claiming otherwise misinforms the public and contributes to an atmosphere of moral panic that risks distracting the national conversation away from important discussions on mental health and gun control.

EVALUATING THE AUTHOR'S ARGUMENTS:

Viewpoint author Christopher J. Ferguson claims that violent video games do not contribute to youth violence. What evidence does he provide to support his claim?

Viewpoint

3

"The evidence is quite clear that youth with disruptive behavior disorders, such as conduct disorder (CD) and attention-deficit hyperactivity disorder (ADHD), manifest substantially increased rates of physically aggressive behavior."

Mental Disorders Are Linked to Youth Aggression and Delinquency

Thomas Grisso

In the following viewpoint Thomas Grisso asserts that there is a link between mental disorders and youth crime and delinquency. Grisso says that anger or aggression can be a symptom of childhood depression, post-traumatic stress disorder, schizophrenia, conduct disorder, and attention deficit/hyperactivity disorder. The risk of aggression associated with these mental disorders means that youth suffering from them are at an increased risk of becoming involved with the juvenile justice system, according to Grisso. Grisso is director of the Law-Psychiatry Program at the University of Massachusetts Medical School.

Thomas Grisso, "Adolescent Offenders with Mental Disorders." From *The Future of Children,* a collaboration of the Woodrow Wilson School of Public and International Affairs at Princeton University and the Brookings Institution." Copyright © 2014 by The Trustees of Princeton University. The Future of Children: A Collaboration of The Woodrow Wilson School of Public and International Affairs at Princeton University and The Brookings Institution. Reproduced with permission.

AS YOU READ, CONSIDER THE FOLLOWING QUESTIONS:
1. What percentage of youth in juvenile justice settings have affective (mood) disorders, according to the author?
2. As explained in the viewpoint, what does *co-morbidity* refer to?
3. What percentage of youth in the community with mental disorders are seriously emotionally disturbed, according to Grisso?

A number of comprehensive studies . . . indicate that certain types of mental disorders are common among youth who are arrested for delinquencies. Indeed, many of the symptoms of these disorders themselves increase the risk of aggression and, therefore, the risk of behavior for which youth are arrested and receive delinquency charges. But the picture that emerges from this research is complex, with some disorders decreasing the risk and others increasing it only in combination with other disorders. The following review captures the broader picture of what is known. . . .

Aggression and Mood Disorders

Research has thoroughly documented an increased tendency toward anger, irritability, and hostility among youth with affective (mood) disorders. Such disorders, mostly various forms of clinical depression, are found in about 10 to 25 percent of youth in juvenile justice settings. Someone not familiar with childhood depression may consider this association odd, since depressed adults frequently appear sad and withdrawn, not angry. But so common is irritability and hostility among youth with depressive disorders that the formal psychiatric definition of childhood depression allows "irritable mood" to be substituted for "depressed mood" as one of the criteria for diagnosing depression in youth. That depressed youth

FAST FACT

About 8 percent of US teens meet the criteria for having a serious emotional disturbance, according to studies funded by the National Institute of Mental Health and published in April 2012.

Research has thoroughly documented an increased tendency toward anger, irritability, and hostility among youth with affective (mood) disorders.

are often sullen and belligerent, rather than simply sad, has a number of implications for aggression in social situations. The irritable mood of such youth increases the likelihood that they will provoke angry responses from other youth (and adults), thus augmenting the risk of events that escalate to physical aggression and result in arrests. . . .

Youth with PTSD [post-traumatic stress disorder] and conduct disorder (a disorder characterized by antisocial tendencies) have been found to be more impulsive and aggressive than youth with conduct disorder alone.

Psychotic disorders such as schizophrenia are fairly rare before early adulthood and are not often seen in juvenile justice settings. Nevertheless, some youth have psychotic-like symptoms, possibly as early forms of the disorder, that include thought disturbances—that is, unusual and sometimes bizarre interpretations of events. The evidence that youth with "evolving" psychotic disorders present a greater threat of aggression than other youth is quite weak. But when youth with psychotic features engage in serious delinquencies, one frequently finds that their disturbed thought has played a role in their aggression.

Conduct Disorder and Attention-Deficit Hyperactivity Disorder

In contrast, the evidence is quite clear that youth with disruptive behavior disorders, such as conduct disorder (CD) and attention-deficit hyperactivity disorder (ADHD), manifest substantially increased rates of physically aggressive behavior. This finding is not surprising, given the features of these disorders. Aggressive and delinquent behaviors are part of the criteria for obtaining a CD diagnosis, and ADHD is diagnosed in part by impulsiveness, which can often lead a youth to respond to emotional situations without pausing to consider the consequences. We cannot simply dismiss conduct disorder as "not really a mental disorder, but merely bad character," because there is considerable evidence that the great majority of youth in the juvenile justice system diagnosed with CD also meet diagnostic criteria for other clinical disorders. . . .

Youth with More than One Mental Disorder

Two other complexities of child disorders have significant implications for policy and practice. The first is co-morbidity, or the presence of more than one mental disorder, which is very common among adolescents with mental disorders. Among youth in juvenile justice

Mental Health Disorders in the Juvenile Justice System

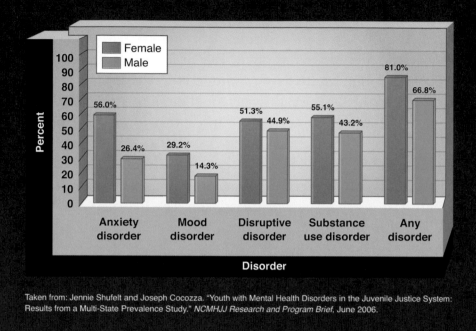

Taken from: Jennie Shufelt and Joseph Cocozza. "Youth with Mental Health Disorders in the Juvenile Justice System: Results from a Multi-State Prevalence Study." *NCMHJJ Research and Program Brief*, June 2006.

facilities who meet criteria for having any mental disorder, about two-thirds meet criteria for two or more disorders.

The second type of clinical complexity with implications for policy and practice involves a class of youth often called "seriously emotionally disturbed." Such youth have multiple mental disorders, manifested from before adolescence, that persist throughout their adolescence and into adulthood. They account for a relatively small proportion of youth in the community with mental disorders (estimated at 10 percent). But the extent of their disabilities is such that they consume nearly half of the community's mental health resources. Almost all of them have juvenile justice contact during their adolescence, and a majority continues to have criminal justice contact—for both minor and serious offenses—as they transition into adulthood.

In summary, research confirms that many specific mental disorders and their co-morbidity increase the risk of aggression because their emotional symptoms (such as anger) and self-regulatory symptoms (such as impulsiveness) themselves increase the risk of aggression. The increased risk of aggression, in turn, increases the risk that youth with these symptoms will be arrested, charged, and convicted of delinquencies and may have continued criminal justice contact as they move into adulthood.

EVALUATING THE AUTHOR'S ARGUMENTS:

How would you describe the tone of Thomas Grisso's viewpoint? For instance, an author may present his or her viewpoint in an authoritative, emotional, or straightforward manner. Which tone do you think is more persuasive?

There Is More than One "System" in Juvenile Justice

"Mental health issues cannot be the main reason young people come into the justice system."

Jeffrey Butts

In the following viewpoint Jeffrey Butts maintains that efforts to prevent juvenile crime should not focus on mental health issues. According to Butts, the effect of mental health issues on juvenile crime is often misunderstood and mischaracterized. Despite the large proportion of youth with mental disorders in secure facilities, mental health is not the main reason youth end up in the juvenile justice system, he notes. Butts says juvenile justice professionals need to appreciate this fact when suggesting policies to reduce youth crime. Butts is director of the Research and Evaluation Center at the John Jay College of Criminal Justice, City University of New York.

AS YOU READ, CONSIDER THE FOLLOWING QUESTIONS:
1. Besides mental health issues, what other issues does Butts say are in the "bundle of issues" affecting public understanding of juvenile crime and justice?

Jeffrey Butts "There Is More than One 'System' in Juvenile Justice," *Juvenile Justice Information Exchange,* April 24, 2013. Reproduced with permission.

2. What fraction of youth have a diagnosable mental health disorder at intake, as demonstrated by Gail Wasserman and her colleagues in the following viewpoint?
3. What percentage of all youth referred to juvenile court end up in secure facilities, according to data from the National Center for Juvenile Justice, as cited by the author?

M ental health is one important issue in a bundle of issues affecting public understanding of juvenile crime and juvenile justice. Others in the same bundle include substance abuse, family violence, head injuries and various forms of trauma. Together, these influence juvenile justice policy and practice in profound ways. They are also easily misunderstood.

Psychologist Gail Wasserman and her colleagues at Columbia University published a study . . . in 2010 showing that mental health disorders are found in larger numbers as researchers look more deeply into the justice system. From intake, to detention and corrections, the prevalence of disorders grows as studies collect mental health screening data at ever-deeper stages of the justice process. By the time researchers analyze prevalence data in the deepest part of the system (secure facilities) mental health and substance abuse disorders affect two-thirds or more of the population.

So, what's the problem? It's the sloppy way that practitioners and policymakers sometimes discuss these findings. Advocates in the mental health sector often characterize such studies as showing that the vast majority of youth in "the juvenile justice system" have diagnosable mental health disorders. Upon hearing this claim, it is natural to infer that mental health problems must be the main reason that young people end up in juvenile justice. Thus, our efforts to prevent and reduce juvenile crime should focus on mental health.

> ## FAST FACT
>
> In 2010 there were 70,792 youth in juvenile detention and correctional facilities in the United States, according to the Annie E. Casey Foundation's Kids Count Data Center.

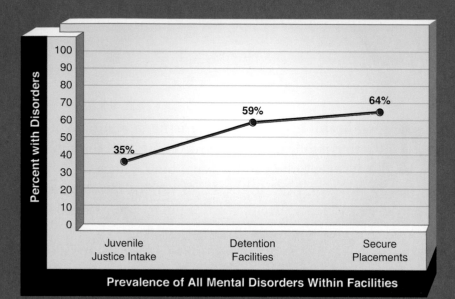

Prevalence of Mental Disorders Increases as Youth Penetrate Justice System

Prevalence of All Mental Disorders Within Facilities

Prevalence estimates for youth at various stages of the juvenile justice process are from Gail A. Wasserman, Larkin S. McReynolds, Craig S. Schwalbe, Joseph M. Keating and Shane A. Jones (2010). "Psychiatric Disorder, Comorbidity, and Suicidal Behavior in Juvenile Justice Youth." *Criminal Justice and Behavior*, 37(12): 1361–1376.

Taken from: Jeffrey Butts, "Mental Health and Drug Disorders Less Common at Early Stages of Juvenile Justice." *Databits*, April 12, 2012.

Mental health issues cannot be the main reason young people come into the justice system if, as Wasserman and her colleagues demonstrated, only one-third of youth at an early stage of justice processing (intake) have any diagnosable disorders. (If we had good mental health screening data at an even earlier stage of processing—i.e., arrest—the number of affected youth would likely be lower and probably closer to the figures found in the general population—15–20 percent.)

Equating the deepest end of juvenile justice with "the system" distorts the significance of whatever problems affect the youth in secure care. Young people in secure facilities represent a small proportion of the entire youthful offender population. We know from national data stored at the National Center for Juvenile Justice that just 20 percent of all youth referred to juvenile court are held in detention for any time at all while awaiting court proceedings, and fewer than 5 percent end up in secure facilities.

An inmate crouches in a crowded detention facility. Despite the high number of mentally disordered youth in juvenile detention, the author argues that mental health issues are not the primary causes of juvenile crime.

The high prevalence rate of mental health disorders in secure facilities suggests that the justice process is likely to divert young people with fewer problems while holding onto those with more problems. This is, in fact, what we want the justice system to do. Service needs in the deep end, however, are not a suitable guide for designing interventions for all youth coming into contact with the larger system. Prevention and early intervention should focus on supportive and restorative services, youth development and skill-building approaches, while services in the deep end should include a stronger focus on mental health and substance abuse. As juvenile justice professionals, we need to pay close attention to our words and to the policy conclusions they may suggest.

EVALUATING THE AUTHOR'S ARGUMENTS:

Viewpoint author Jeffrey Butts says that juvenile justice experts need to be careful about the way they discuss data on the prevalence of mental health disorders in the juvenile justice system. Consider Butts's opinion and go back and read Thomas Grisso's opinion in the previous viewpoint. Do you think Butts would agree with the way Grisso has presented data on mental health issues in the juvenile justice system?

School Violence Is Linked to Bullying

Courtney Parker

"And then a light bulb turns on. You realize the shooter was the victim of continuous bullying that sparked a dangerous and life-threatening but avoidable situation."

In the following viewpoint Courtney Parker contends that the prevalence of tragic school shootings could be reduced if more attention were paid to bullying prevention. Parker says that youth who are bullied take vengeance on their bullies and other students as a way to try to regain control of their lives. In order to prevent school shootings, teachers, parents, other adults, and other students need to reach out to the victims of bullying, says Parker. Parker is a writer for the University of California–Riverside newspaper, the *Highlander*.

AS YOU READ, CONSIDER THE FOLLOWING QUESTIONS:

1. According to Parker, on average, how many junior high schools, high schools, and colleges are affected by school violence each year?
2. Since the Columbine High School massacre in April 1999, how many school shootings have there been, according to an article on PolicyMic?
3. Does Parker think those convicted of mass murder who have been bullied should be given more lenient sentences?

Courtney Parker, "The Cause and Solution of School Violence, and How We Can End the Cycle of Bullying," *Highlander News,* January 29, 2013. Copyright © 2013 by Highlander News. All rights Reserved. Reproduced by permission.

Whe it happens, you don't even realize it. Just a brief, surreal moment that could turn out to be a dream. You couldn't see the horror coming. A booming sound comes from down the hallway that almost sounds as if a firework has been accidently set off. And then you see blood, yellow caution tape, paramedics with stretchers, cops with guns and handcuffs, and then, the horrifying discovery that your classmate has been shot by another classmate. You think to yourself, "What happened? What was this person thinking? True, he wasn't the most popular kid in school. . . ." And then a light bulb turns on. You realize the shooter was the victim of continuous bullying that sparked a dangerous and life-threatening but avoidable situation.

School violence is an unfortunately common issue that affects an average of five junior high schools, high schools and college campuses every year. The various reasons and causes of these tragic epidemics stem from many sources, particularly mental illness and bullying.

Bullying Is All Too Common

But despite its known correlation with violence in schools, bullying is one problem that is not discussed as much as it needs to be. Bullying, harassment and intimidation are linked to 75 percent of school shootings. This particular issue connected to school violence can often be ignored because of the victim's fear or people's own negligence.

In a 2011 study conducted by the Centers for Disease Control and Prevention (CDC), 20 percent of students in grades nine through 12 reported being bullied within the grounds of their school, while 16 percent of the students reported being cyber-bullied. There are millions of children and teenagers who are bullied every year, yet these percentages only reflect the reported cases of bullying.

These statistics cover only reported cases, but it's reasonable to suspect that the percentages are in fact much higher. The proportions may not seem incredibly large, but the problem still exists and will continue to exist unless serious actions are taken by the people who can create the most change, including school board representatives and higher-level government figures.

School Violence Motivated by Bullying

According to an article on *PolicyMic.com*, there have been 31 school shootings since the infamous Columbine High School Massacre in

Historically, bullying, harassment, and intimidation have been linked to 75 percent of school shootings.

April 1999 [in which two students killed one teacher, twelve students, and themselves]. Included within these horrific acts of mass murder is the Virginia Tech Massacre in 2007 [in which the shooter killed thirty-two people and himself in two separate attacks], which is the deadliest school shooting by a single gunman in United States history.

Virginia Tech was also an incident motivated by bullying. The shooter, Seung-Hui Cho, suffered a great deal of bullying from his high school classmates prior to attending Virginia Tech. Cho was constantly mocked and laughed at in high school because of his quiet nature, shyness and difficulty speaking English. This example alone is just one scenario out of many that have resulted in a tragedy that could have been prevented.

Cho's unfortunate history of being bullied was a contributing factor to the grisly deeds committed six years ago [in 2007]. He, along with many other shooters, was abused and intimidated by cruelty and oppression.

Aside from the humiliation, many quiet and shy students like Cho did not receive, and still don't receive, enough help or guidance from teachers and other administrative staff. Even though Cho chose not to talk to a counselor, more of his past instructors should have recognized Cho's unusually quiet behavior and lack of social aptitude in order to help him through the continuous bullying.

Bullying Victims Seek to Regain Control with Vengeance

Being bullied and mocked by anybody creates a weakness within an individual—a loss of confidence so to speak. The longer the harassment lasts, the more of a toll it takes on one's emotions and sense of self. The victim wants to regain some, if not all, of the control that was lost because of the horrendous treatment.

This is where violent and bloody vengeance comes into play. When someone is bullied, they are being victimized and tortured. Victims of bullying may experience physical harm and even death threats from their fellow peers. Unable to face humiliation forever, those bullied think of revenge, and those who caused the distress and torment among their victims are usually the ones that are placed on the shooter's "hit list". In the mind of the would-be shooter, taking the life of a bully takes away the bully's power.

FAST FACT

According to the US Department of Health and Human Services website StopBullying.gov, in twelve of fifteen school shooting cases in the 1990s, the shooters had a history of being bullied.

Helping the Bullied to Prevent Tragedy

But even if those convicted of mass murder have been bullied, they should not be given more lenient sentences. Anybody can sympathize with a victim of bullying, but the actions taken were completely intentional and premeditated. Victims of bullying should have other outlets and resources to ease their fear and sadness. Teachers, guidance counselors and the people who witness bullying or are made aware of it must be the ones who direct the victims in the right direction. Control over one's life due can be reclaimed through counseling and

Homicides by Students on School Grounds During the School Day: 1992–1993 to 2010

The rate of homicides in US schools has declined substantially since the early 1990s. There was an apparent interruption in the downward trend during a period of highly publicized shootings that may have generated some copycat shootings.

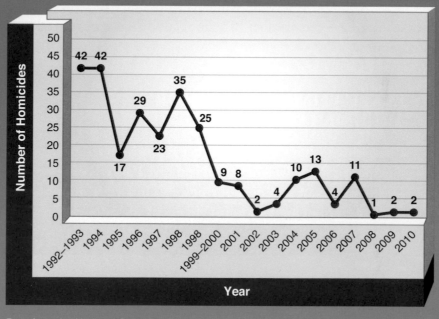

Data from the National School Safety Center

Taken from: Youth Violence Project. Curry School of Education. http://curry.virginia.edu/research/projects/violence -in-schools/national-statistics.

talking to a trusted individual. Even the victim talking directly to the bully can help regain control over the victim's life.

Intending harm upon another is a permanent and detrimental solution to an avoidable and temporary problem. Revisiting the source of the shooter's revenge—reclaiming control—can be resolved through healthier methods in order to cease bullying. The best resource is an adult. Unfortunately, people may not pick up on the warning signs of the victim's pain until it is too late. In order to control the horror of bullying, teachers, parents, counselors, and other students need to express concern and compassion toward the victims of bullying, because the power of just one helping hand can be the difference between peace and tragedy.

One in seven students in Kindergarten through 12th grade has either been a bully or have been bullied. Considering that statistic alone, this is what we need to remember: bullying can happen anywhere, anytime, in any school, to any student. We must recognize the attacks early on, and intervene whenever possible. Just these actions alone can decrease the number of school shootings committed in the United States.

EVALUATING THE AUTHOR'S ARGUMENTS:

Viewpoint author Courtney Parker is a writer for a college newspaper. What weight would you give Parker's opinion on the causes of school shootings? Would your opinion of the weight of her viewpoint change if she or one of her loved ones was a victim of bullying? Explain.

How to Deal with Guns in School

> *"The presence of weapons and toleration of them on campus create the potential for more pain and suffering in the nation's schools."*

Ron Avi Astor

In the following viewpoint Ron Avi Astor asserts that doing something to reduce the numbers of gun-packing students on school grounds would help prevent school shootings. According to Astor, the number of weapons, including guns and knives, on school campuses is a major problem. Astor thinks teachers and school administrators need to ask students how prevalent weapons are and then use the information to reduce the presence of guns in schools. Astor is a professor in urban social development at the University of Southern California. He is also coauthor of the book *School Violence in Context*.

AS YOU READ, CONSIDER THE FOLLOWING QUESTIONS:

1. According to Astor, the results of the 2009–2011 California Healthy Kids Survey indicate what percentage of fifth-grade students bring a weapon to school?
2. What percentage of secondary school students in California and nationwide report being threatened with a weapon, according to the author?
3. As stated in the viewpoint, what did a 2008 report published by the American Psychological Association indicate about the effectiveness of zero-tolerance measures to make schools safer?

Rov Avi Astor "How to Deal with Guns in School," CNN.com, December 21, 2012. From CNN.com, December 21, 2012. Copyright © 2012 by Cable News Network, Inc. All rights reserved. Used by permission and protected by the Copyright Laws of the United States. The printing, copying, redistribution, or retransmission of this Content without express written permission is prohibited.

Last week's massacre at Sandy Hook Elementary School in Newtown, Connecticut, appears to have at least temporarily changed the debate on gun control and opened the door to new restrictions.

Following up on his pledge to "use whatever power this office holds" to prevent another slaughter at a school, President Barack Obama has said he will submit new gun-restriction proposals to Congress in January. But the obstacles to progress remain formidable, chief among them the political power of the gun-rights lobby in Washington.

Yet we don't have to wait until the national gun-control debate plays out to better protect our children from violence at school.

We can begin now in our elementary and secondary schools by starting a campaign to eliminate the number of lethal weapons that students bring to campus. Despite laws against them and some progress in reducing their numbers, weapons on campus continue to be a major problem.

FAST FACT

According to the Youth Risk Behavior Survey for 2011, Massachusetts had the lowest percentage of high school students reporting they carried a gun (2.5 percent), and Wyoming had the highest (10.8 percent).

Over the past decade, various government agencies have surveyed millions of students across the nation about weapons in schools, and, year after year, they have told us that they have seen guns and knives on campus and have been threatened by them at school. Alarmingly, a sizable minority don't disapprove of them being on school grounds. The presence of weapons and toleration of them on campus create the potential for more pain and suffering in the nation's schools. According to the most recent federal statistics, there were 33 school-associated violent deaths from July 1, 2009, through June 30, 2010.

"Nationwide," reports the most recent Centers for Disease Control and Prevention's Youth Risk Behavior Survey, "5.4% of students had carried a weapon (e.g., a gun, knife or club) on school property on at least one day during the 30 days before the survey."

Shooter Adam Lanza's weapons found at Sandy Hook Elementary are shown. Surveys suggest that hundreds of thousands of potentially lethal weapons are being smuggled onto the nation's school grounds.

Data from the 2009–2011 California Healthy Kids Survey, the most recent, show a horrifying number of weapons-packing students. About 5% of secondary-school students said they carried a firearm to campus, while another 10% reported bringing knives and other potentially lethal weapons during the past year. Stunningly, about 3% of fifth-graders reported that they brought a weapon to school.

Taken together, the surveys suggest that hundreds of thousands of potentially lethal weapons are being smuggled onto the nation's school grounds—and students may be using them for self-protection but also to threaten their classmates. Around 8% of secondary-school students in California and nationally report such threats in recent surveys, a percentage that has stayed basically unchanged since 1993.

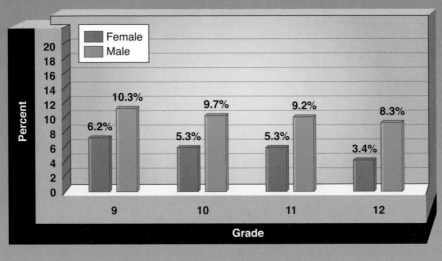

Students Threatened or Injured with a Weapon on School Property, 2011

Female
Male

Percent

20
18
16
14
12
10
8
6
4
2
0

6.2%
10.3%
5.3%
9.7%
5.3%
9.2%
3.4%
8.3%

9   10   11   12

Grade

Taken from: Centers for Disease Control and Prevention. Youth Risk Behavior Surveillance—United States, 2011. *Morbidity and Mortality Weekly Report 2012*, vol. 61, no. 4..

Even if not directly threatened with a weapon, many students are nonetheless aware of the presence of guns and knives on their campus. For about a decade now, about one-quarter to one-third of students in California public schools (both elementary and secondary) and other states have reported such awareness.

In past decades, schools have installed metal detectors, hired extra security to patrol grounds and hallways and instituted other zero-tolerance measures to make campuses safer. But a report released by a zero-tolerance task force assembled and published by the American Psychological Association in 2008 concluded there was no evidence that these measures were effective in making students and staff feel safer. And they can be self-defeating: It's tough to learn or feel cared for in a prison-like setting.

So what to do?

For starters, we should listen to what the students are telling us in the surveys. Yes, listen, because few in our schools, communities and government are. How can you reduce weapons in schools if you do not know what students think about guns in school and you have no clear idea of just how prevalent the problem is?

Step one is for teachers and principals to use the survey results from their own states—in California the data is available online—to open discussions with students and parents about the presence of weapons on campus and their potential use as a threat. The many students in California and other states who think there's nothing wrong with weapons being in students' backpacks need to learn that what they may see in society at large—the presence of guns in many places—is unacceptable on school grounds.

As important as changing their attitudes toward weapons on campus is providing students with anonymous ways to let authorities know about a potential threat. Schools that have created such channels of communication report that the information has thwarted many incidents over the past decade.

The best prevention of student-instigated violence on campus is an educated, well-trained and caring school community in which everyone understands what to do when they see a weapon on campus and why it might save lives to act. We can begin to build such a community by talking with students in each classroom and each school about what they see, hear and experience while at school.

Ignoring students' voices won't save lives.

EVALUATING THE AUTHOR'S ARGUMENTS:

Viewpoint author Ron Avi Astor contends that weapons are widespread on school campuses and that reducing the number of these weapons would help prevent school violence. What evidence does he provide to support the link between the availability of weapons in schools and school violence?

Chapter 2

How Should the Criminal Justice System Treat Juvenile Offenders?

Society is divided on whether to incarcerate juvenile offenders as adults.

Should Juvenile Criminals Be Sentenced Like Adults?

Clark Merrefield

"Available research shows that prosecuting young people as adults does not rehabilitate them or deter future crimes."

In the following viewpoint Clark Merrefield chronicles South Carolina teen Sean Shevlino's progression from a typical American teen to an inmate in state prison. When Shevlino was sixteen years old, he and his friends committed armed robbery at a grocery store. According to Merrefield, South Carolina law required that Shevlino be sentenced as an adult, and he received ten years in the state prison. Merrefield says that attitudes about sentencing juveniles like Shevlino as adults are changing, because science has revealed that adolescent brains are still developing. According to Merrefield, sentencing juveniles as adults costs more money and does not prevent future crimes or rehabilitate young offenders. Merrefield is a journalist who has written for *Newsweek* and the Daily Beast. He was a 2012 Juvenile Justice Journalism Fellow at John Jay College.

Clark Merrefield, "Should Juvenile Criminals Be Sentenced Like Adults?," Daily Beast, November 26, 2012. Reproduced with permission.

AS YOU READ, CONSIDER THE FOLLOWING QUESTIONS:
1. When Shevlino spoke to the Daily Beast by phone from the MacDougall Correctional Institution, how many years into his ten-year sentence was he?
2. What ages, roughly, are the worst time in a person's life for rational decision making, according to the author?
3. According to Merrefield, how much money would North Carolina save if the age to sentence a teen as an adult for misdemeanors and nonviolent felonies was moved from sixteen to eighteen?

I n August 2006, Sean Shevlino pulled on a hoodie, went to a Piggly Wiggly near his house, waited until the coast was clear, and hopped the counter.

Sean's friend's older brother worked at the Piggly Wiggly, and had told Sean that when the lady behind the service counter went for a smoke break, all Sean had to do was jump over and snag some cash from the safe. It wouldn't be locked.

Sure enough, it wasn't. Sean opened the safe, grabbed a Ziploc bag of cash, stuffed it under his hoodie, and ran to a friend's house. He was 16.

Before then, Sean had seemed to be a typical American kid from Mount Pleasant, S.C., a politically conservative, affluent suburb outside Charleston. He was the quiet, introverted brother between Seamus and Alex. His mother, April, was a schoolteacher; his father, Peter, is a Navy veteran who leases shipping containers. Peter and April provided what they felt was a comfortable, college-bound track for the boys. Life seemed as normal as it gets.

But when Sean turned 15, "things quickly went downhill," April said. "He started acting terrible to us. He just seemed very angry."

Sean was couch surfing with friends before the robbery, and had been looking for a quick way to pay his friends back for their hospitality.

When Sean told them about the idea to rob the Piggly Wiggly, they told him he was crazy. But when Sean got an idea in his head, it stuck.

"When I got all the money, [my friends'] minds changed a little bit," Sean said.

And then Sean and his buddies had another idea: if he could get that much money again, maybe even more, they could get their own apartment. A few of the friends were 18 and could sign a lease. Sean would still go to school and finish his education, but he'd live on his terms.

The Food Lion just off Highway 17 was bigger than the Piggly Wiggly. It would have more money. Easy money, part two.

But the boys soon realized that the Food Lion had more fail-safes; it wouldn't be as simple as hopping a counter. Someone—Sean doesn't remember who—suggested using a toy gun to stick up the place. Sean thought about it for half a second. "Yeah, why not?" he said. "We can do that.

With the last of the Piggly Wiggly cash, the teens bought their supplies: an orange ski mask, a pair of motorcycle gloves, a pellet gun, four walkie talkies, and a pair of goggles.

Just before 11 PM on Aug. 26, the plan coalesced.

Sean—whose code name was "Butch Cassidy"—crouched below a big window near the Food Lion's entrance. Christopher Cousins, 16, who worked at the store, said over the radios, "Butch is about to do it."

As the last customer left the store, Sean recalled, Chris said, "If you're gonna do it, Sean, you gotta do it right now."

Sean could hear doubt in Chris's voice. "Nobody really thought we were going to go through with this thing," Sean said. "I heard that and I had this thought—I didn't really want to do it—but I had all these expectations riding on my shoulders. I had gotten them all involved in it up to this point."

Nobody backed down.

Sean entered the Food Lion. He found a manager who was buying a package of Goldfish crackers and pulled the pellet gun on him.

"He was terrified," Sean said. "And that's when it hit me. Like, Oh my God, I just scared the crap out of this guy."

With the pellet gun pointed at him the manager opened the safe. Sean packed a black gym bag with as much cash as he could grab, and then he and the lookouts bolted across the parking lot to the getaway car, a blue-green Toyota RAV4.

"Haul ass!" Sean told the driver, Graham Stolte.

Stolte pulled onto Highway 17 and blue lights appeared out of the darkness. The police were flying toward the Food Lion.

"Holy shit," Sean thought as the cop cars streaked by in the opposite direction. "I just did something serious right here. I shouldn't have done that."

When the cash was counted there was nowhere near enough for Sean to get an apartment, and the money soon ran out. About a week later—after another robbery and a BMW joyride—the police caught up with Sean. Eleven teenagers in all, including the starting quarterback at the local high school, were involved to varying degrees with the two-week crime spree.

Sitting in an interrogation room, Peter Shevlino asked his son if he had really stolen a car. He knew Sean had been acting out, but he never expected anything like this.

"Yeah," Sean said. "I did."

Peter ran his hands through his hair and looked at Sean without speaking.

"When he didn't yell at me that's when I knew I had really messed up," Sean said.

Sean, now 22, spoke to *The Daily Beast* by phone from MacDougall Correctional Institution in Ridgeville, S.C., five years into a 10-year sentence for armed robbery. Under South Carolina law, Sean, who was 16 at the time of his crimes, was charged as an adult.

FAST FACT

According to US Department of Justice statistics, on any given night in America ten thousand children are held in adult jails and prisons.

Increasingly, social scientists, law-enforcement authorities, lawyers, and judges are questioning the wisdom of charging juveniles as adults.

It is only in the last few years that the law has begun to recognize what science has long known: that adolescent brain development takes more time than previously thought.

"While some teenagers can be astonishingly mature and others inconceivably childish, middle adolescence—roughly, ages 14 to 18—might be the worst time in a person's life for rational decision mak-

Sean Shevlino and his fellow students are arraigned in a Charleston, South Carolina, court for robbing a food store. Statistics reveal that a quarter-million teenagers under eighteen pass through the adult criminal justice system each year.

ing," says Laurence Steinberg, an adolescent psychologist at Temple University. Research has repeatedly shown that during these years, pleasure centers are at full throttle, and foresight is lacking, particularly in young men.

"Among all American boys, about 75 percent violate the law at some point," Steinberg says. "For some it might be as minor as possession of marijuana and for others it could be as serious as armed robbery, but in either case they're breaking the law. The question we ask is why some stop and others don't. Our sense is most stop because they just grow up."

During pre- and early-adolescence, the brain becomes more efficient and logical, and dopamine activity increases. Things like sex, drugs, and adrenaline thrills feel really good, and when teens are in groups they are even more likely to go for the thrill.

But as teens approach adulthood, the pathways between the brain's CEO and the limbic system—the emotional center—increase substantially, allowing for greater impulse control. According to some studies, brain development is not complete until the mid-20s.

Steinberg is concerned that harsh punishment of juveniles often doesn't fit the crime. "If it were just a process of normal maturation, then I think it's important that we don't sanction them in a way that's going to mess up their lives."

Sean's original prosecutor offered him the 10-year sentence—in an adult prison—as part of a plea deal. But the Shevlinos resisted, hoping that if Sean could demonstrate an ability to change, maybe the new prosecutor, Scarlett Wilson, would reduce the charges and offer a youthful offender sentence.

The plan was that Sean would hold off on accepting the plea for as long as possible. In the meantime he would go to Three Springs, a now-defunct Outward Bound–style program in middle-of-nowhere Pittsboro, N.C. He'd learn how to control his anger and defiance. (After a battery of psychological tests, Sean had been diagnosed with oppositional defiant disorder).

In early October 2006 Sean spent his first night at Three Springs. He had to prove that even though his actions belied a simmering anger, he wasn't one of the violent ones. More than that, Sean had to show he could lead among his regiment of 12 boys.

Sean moved swiftly through the military-style hierarchy, and by the end of his time was performing the work of paid counselors. The Three Springs program certainly wasn't a cure-all for every young man, but for some, like Sean, it seemed to work. It helped him learn to manage his ODD and prepare to reenter society.

But in the heart of tough-on-crime country, there was a public perception that an example had to be made. Wilson, the prosecutor, explained that she ultimately decided the 10-year plea deal was appropriate for Sean and one of the other teens—the two "ringleaders."

Sean had to make a choice: go to trial and face decades in prison, or take the plea. Sean accepted the plea in January 2008. With good behavior he would be out of adult prison in eight and a half years.

According to one frequently quoted statistic, a quarter-million teenagers under 18 pass through the adult justice system each year. Howard Snyder, a researcher with the Bureau of Justice Statistics, is developing a more statistically rigorous estimate using a sampling of court cases from 2012. But right now, even he isn't exactly sure how many juveniles encounter the adult system each year.

What Snyder does know is that 40 percent of 17-year-olds in America do not have any chance to be tried as a juvenile, and the available research shows that prosecuting young people as adults does not

Youth Under Eighteen in Adult Prisons, 2009

The Bureau of Justice Statistics reported that approximately 2,778 youth under age eighteen were held in custody in adult state prisons in 2009.

State	Number of Youths
Maine	0
New Hampshire	0
North Dakota	0
Kentucky	0
West Virginia	0
California	0
Idaho	0
Rhode Island	0
South Dakota	1
Montana	1
Wyoming	1
Hawaii	2
Washington	2
New Mexico	3
Vermont	4
Kansas	5
Utah	6
Alaska	7
Massachusetts	8
Iowa	13
Minnesota	13
Oregon	13
Louisiana	15
Virginia	16
Arkansas	17
Oklahoma	19
New Jersey	21
Nebraska	21
Tennessee	22
Delaware	28
Mississippi	28
Missouri	31
Wisconsin	37
Indiana	54
Maryland	58
Pennsylvania	61
Colorado	79
Ohio	86
South Carolina	89
Georgia	99
Illinois	106
Alabama	118
Nevada	118
Michigan	156
Texas	156
Arizona	157
New York	190
North Carolina	215
Connecticut	332
Florida	393
United States	2,778

Taken from: Children's Defense Fund. *The State of America's Children Handbook*, 2012.

rehabilitate them or deter future crimes. A U.S. Department of Justice review of several large-scale studies found that, excluding arrests for nonviolent property or drug offenses, young people tried in adult criminal court generally have greater recidivism rates than those tried in juvenile court.

However, recent Supreme Court cases and new state legislation indicate a changing attitude toward how we treat our youngest wrong-doers.

In 2005 the court outlawed the death penalty for those who had committed their crimes before the age of 18, relying in large part on the emerging science of brain development. The court went a step further last summer, prohibiting mandatory sentences of life without parole for juveniles. Also since 2005, several states have raised the adult criminal bar to age 18, either for some or all offenses. A state task force in North Carolina, one of two states where the age of criminal responsibility is 16, has recommended that for minor crimes, teens under 18 remain in the juvenile system.

The benefits of keeping juveniles out of the adult system are also financial. If the age were raised to 18 for misdemeanors and nonviolent felonies, North Carolina would net $52.3 million a year over the long run, according to an analysis by the Vera Institute of Justice.

Sean Shevlino is now an adult, but he spent the last years of his youth in the same prison where he now sits. The experience has no doubt affected him deeply, and has changed his father's views on criminal justice too.

"I never believed in my wildest dreams that children were treated like this in this country," Peter Shevlino said. "You would have called me a hard-right, conservative Republican. The people in that camp—even after this, very good friends that we have—they still cling to the idea that this is sort of a one-off. It's hard for people to accept that, no, it's not, we have a severely broken system. It's hard to accept that everything we've been doing for the past 40 to 50 years has been wrong."

Even Scarlett Wilson explained by email that while she has no control over legislation, she believes "it is better when juveniles are housed in prison separately from adults."

After Sean accepted his 10-year sentence, he was taken by bus to Kirkland maximum security prison in Columbia, S.C. He looked up at the sentry towers dotting the campus as the bus entered Kirkland. He couldn't believe what was happening.

"You get to Kirkland and you get stripped naked and they wash you down and you're with all these people—like 50 or 60 guys—and I'm the youngest one there by far," Sean said. "I'm just looking around like, There's no way I could ever do 10 years here in prison. That's not going to happen."

Sean had to fight other inmates, especially early on, but the work he did at Three Springs and consistent contact with his family have helped him maintain perspective and adapt to prison.

"I've seen a lot of young guys like me who didn't have a head on their shoulders and didn't know how to handle the pressure," he said. "Back here it's survival of the fittest."

EVALUATING THE AUTHOR'S ARGUMENTS:

Why do you think viewpoint author Clark Merrefield tells Sean Shevlino's story? Do you think Shevlino's story makes Merrefield's viewpoint stronger or weaker? Explain.

"All crimes committed by juveniles should and must be treated in the same regard, if not to punish heinous acts, then to provide justice to the families of victims."

Adult Punishment Should Be an Option for Juvenile Offenders

Jessica Wilde

In the following viewpoint Jessica Wilde contends that juveniles who commit heinous crimes should not be treated differently than adults. Wilde discusses two cases involving child murderers: eleven-year-old Jordan Brown from Pennsylvania and the two ten-year-old-murderers of toddler Jamie Bulger in England. Wilde does not think rehabilitation of these juvenile killers is even an issue. They should be sentenced as adults to punish their despicable acts and to provide justice to the victims' families, says Wilde. At the time this article was written, Wilde was a writer for the *Rebel Yell*, the newspaper of the University of Nevada–Las Vegas.

Jessica Wilde, "Juvenile Criminals Must Be Tried as Adults," *The Rebel Yell*, March 5, 2009. Copyright © 2009 by The Rebel Yell. All Rights Reserved. Reproduced with permission.

1. According to Wilde, what does the National Center for Juvenile Justice Profiles say is the reason juveniles should be treated differently from adult criminals?
2. According to Wilde, what happened to the ten-year-old killers of Jamie Bulger?
3. What does Wilde want those who advocate for a second chance for youths to think about?

In light of 11-year-old Jordan Brown [from New Castle, Pennsylvania] murdering his father's pregnant girlfriend [in 2009] because he was "jealous" and thankfully being tried by Pennsylvania's court system as an adult, one may ask, why don't juveniles committing crimes so heinous get the punishment they deserve more often?

This child, among countless others who commit crimes such as rape, robbery, assault, murder and attempted murder are exempt from being tried in a criminal trial purely because of their age. The National Center for Juvenile Justice Profiles explains that juveniles are treated differently from adult criminals because "youth behavior is malleable" and can be reformed with treatment and successful rehabilitation.

The privacy of minors is protected during the hearing and they are never referred to as guilty—only as delinquent. Criminal trials differ in that all court proceedings are available to the public and defendants are found simply innocent or guilty based on the facts.

FAST FACT

According to the Centers for Disease Control and Prevention, 784 juveniles (persons under age eighteen) were arrested for murder in the United States in 2010.

No Excuses for Juvenile Killers

The obvious problem in trying minors as minors and not treating them in the same way for the same crimes is that rehabilitation will not fix these young criminals. It is simply not important if the children can be

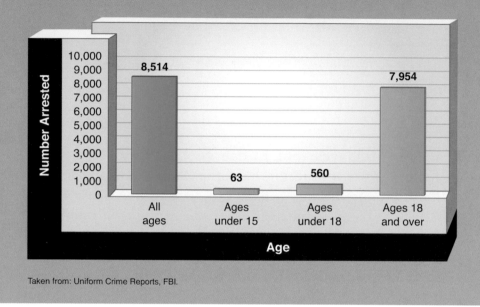

Age of Those Arrested for Murder and Nonnegligent Manslaughter, 2012

Taken from: Uniform Crime Reports, FBI.

rehabilitated and fixed into not being repeat offenders. Prevention of relapse should not be the main focus because situations like this should never arise in the first place.

In 1993, 2-year-old Jamie Bulger living in Bootle, England, was taken by two 10-year-old boys and was mutilated and murdered. The two boys then laid his body on a railroad track with the intention of causing substantial injury which would cover up what they had done to the child. The murderers were tried and convicted as minors and the boys have since been relocated and given new identities.

Excuses should not be made for these offenders; lessening the consequences of their actions will not only undermine the victim and his or her family, but also make it seem excusable after a short period of remorse.

A lack of human morals cannot be treated or cured in rehabilitation centers. Morals are inherent from birth, the acknowledgement of right from wrong and the respect of following those lines are unchangeable foundations a person is built upon from the beginning. People either have morals or they don't: there is no gray area. One may argue that morals are evident in one situation but not the other. Does this mean that one can pick and choose when they follow their moral compass, when they should believe in right from wrong?

Some may argue that minors do not understand the significance of their actions, that they don't understand the enormity of what they have done or how it has hurt others. In the case of Bulger, it was reported that the two boys set out that morning with the intention of hurting or killing a young child for fun. They were seen on CCTV [closed-circuit TV] scoping out their victim, and found Bulger when he wandered out of the store where his mother was shopping.

Think of the Victim's Family

To those who advocate a second chance for youths, I have something for you to think about. Put yourself in Bulger's mother's shoes. Would you feel your son's brutal murder was vindicated if the two boys who killed your son, purely for fun, were taken to juvenile detention, received rehabilitative aid and released with new identities to live the rest of their lives with nothing but a faint memory of what they had done? I think not.

All crimes committed by juveniles should and must be treated in the same regard, if not to punish heinous acts, then to provide justice to the families of victims.

EVALUATING THE AUTHOR'S ARGUMENTS:

Would you describe the tone of Jessica Wilde's viewpoint as authoritarian, emotional, or logical? Do you think her argument is persuasive? Why or why not?

There Should Be a Minimum Age for Juvenile Justice

"We do not truly know the short- or long-term personal and emotional effects of bringing young children into the juvenile justice system."

H. Ted Rubin

In the following viewpoint H. Ted Rubin asserts that children should not enter the juvenile justice system until they are at least ten years old. According to Rubin, the effects of being brought into the system on young children could be devastating. Young children also cannot assert their rights, and many do not even understand court proceedings, says Rubin. He believes there are better ways than the juvenile court system to deal with juvenile offenders younger than ten. Rubin is a former juvenile judge and Colorado state legislator. He has authored several books on juvenile justice.

AS YOU READ, CONSIDER THE FOLLOWING QUESTIONS:

1. According to Rubin, which state has the lowest minimum age for bringing children into the juvenile justice system?
2. According to the author, it is likely that many lawyers find it more expedient to arrange a plea bargain rather than do what?
3. As stated in the viewpoint, what is the minimum age for bringing children into the juvenile system across Canada?

H. Ted Rubin,"The Case for a Minimum Age in Juvenile Justice," Youthtoday.org, August 1, 2011. Copyright © 2011 by H.Ted Rubin. All rights reserved. Reproduced with permission.

There has been important and productive attention to increasing the maximum jurisdictional age for juvenile offenders to one's 18th birthday. It is well known that Connecticut has led this effort by raising this age from one's 16th birthday to a 17th birthday maximum effective 2010 and an 18th birthday maximum effective 2012.

Illinois and Mississippi have also recently expanded jurisdictional eligibility a year to the 18th birthday, Illinois for misdemeanors and Mississippi for most felonies. Other states such as Wisconsin and Massachusetts continue to examine jumping their maximum age by a year to 18. Far more states are re-examining provisions of their codes to make it more difficult to transfer serious or chronic offenders, and others are expanding the use of juvenile detention instead of jail detention for youths who are in the criminal court process.

> **FAST FACT**
>
> According to statistics from the US Department of Justice, in 2009 ten- to fourteen-year-olds were most often referred to the juvenile justice system for crimes against persons (21 percent)—including murder, rape, and assault—followed by property crimes (16 percent).

State Minimum Age Provisions

But it is difficult to find states that are looking hard at minimum age provisions. That should change.

Currently, North Carolina has the lowest minimum of just six years of age. Its pending legislative bills to increase its upper age nonetheless maintain the six-year jurisdictional minimum. Next up at the low end are three states—Maryland, Massachusetts, and New York—whose statutes open the juvenile court's delinquency door for those seven years of age. Arizona comes in next at eight years of age.

The more common denominator of ten years is set forth in statutes in such states as Arkansas, Colorado, Kansas, Louisiana, Minnesota, Mississippi, Pennsylvania, South Dakota, Texas, Vermont, and Wisconsin.

But the clear majority of states are silent as to this matter. Presumably, police officers or other complainants in those jurisdictions may ask a juvenile court to bring charges against a child of any age.

The author argues that children younger than ten should not be tried as adults.

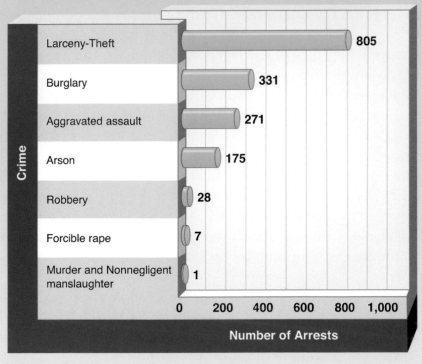

Children Under Ten Arrested in 2012 in the United States

Crime	Number of Arrests
Larceny-Theft	805
Burglary	331
Aggravated assault	271
Arson	175
Robbery	28
Forcible rape	7
Murder and Nonnegligent manslaughter	1

Taken from: Federal Bureau of Investigation. Uniform Crime Reports. www.fbi.gov.

Why a Minimum Age Is Needed

Why is a minimum jurisdictional age of at least ten years an imperative? We do not truly know the short- or long-term personal and emotional effects of bringing young children into the juvenile justice system. This can be a life-changing and negative event, altering how youths see themselves and how they are thereafter seen by family, friends, and school officials. I posit that we can find better ways in the community, and without the court, to reorient these mostly modest offending youngsters while assisting them and their families.

Young juveniles are also at a serious disadvantage as to asserting their rights, unless a state law or case decision requires parental presence during a police interrogation and advisement stage. Law enforcement could better fulfill its protection and service mission with young juveniles by facilitating responsible juvenile-family dialogue and, as appropriate, a carefully facilitated juvenile-family referral to a community service entity.

Juvenile competency to stand trial and assist counsel is another concern. I would presume that myriad young juveniles do not have a significant factual or rational understanding of court proceedings and the consequences they might experience, and many lack the ability to materially aid their lawyers. Likely, many lawyers find it expedient to arrange a plea bargain/disposition with prosecutors rather than secure evaluations that might indicate an inability on the part of the child to proceed. And still, even today, thousands of court youth do not have lawyers who might even consider this concern.

As a state legislator, I successfully lobbied a ten-year minimum jurisdictional age provision into Colorado's statute many years ago, along with a minimum age of twelve-years for commitment to a state delinquency institution. The ten-year minimum still stands, although the commitment minimum age requirement was amended out some years ago.

Across Canada, the minimum age for juvenile court jurisdiction is twelve years of age. This, truly, would be my preference. National U.S. data show that juveniles twelve years of age and under comprise less than eight percent of delinquency referrals.

Whether it is 12 or 10, we do need to legislate a minimum age, and rearrange the system accordingly. The juvenile court should not be the first stop-shop for these young people.

EVALUATING THE AUTHOR'S ARGUMENTS:

Viewpoint author H. Ted Rubin is a former juvenile court judge. What impact do you think this has on the strength of his viewpoint? Explain.

Viewpoint

4

Supreme Court Bars Mandatory Life Sentences for Juveniles

Warren Richey

"The high court declared that automatically sentencing someone so young to a lifetime behind bars . . . is cruel and unusual punishment."

Warren Richey is a staff writer for the *Christian Science Monitor*. In the following viewpoint Richey reports on the ruling by the US Supreme Court that prohibits mandatory life sentences without parole for juvenile offenders. The court ruled such mandatory sentencing constituted cruel and unusual punishment and so violated the Eighth Amendment of the Constitution. A sentence of life without parole is not prohibited, but courts must consider the youthfulness of the offender and any mitigating circumstances before imposing such a sentence.

AS YOU READ, CONSIDER THE FOLLOWING QUESTIONS:

1. As stated by the author, what ruling did Justices Breyer and Sotomayor favor?
2. According to the viewpoint, what rationale was used to arrive at the decision to prohibit mandatory life without parole sentences? What other cases used the same rationale?
3. As stated in the article, which Justice wrote a dissenting opinion, and what was the argument in the dissent?

Warren Richey, "Supreme Court Bars Mandatory Life Sentences for Juveniles," *Christian Science Monitor*, June 25, 2012. Copyright © 2012 by The Christian Science Monitor. All rights reserved. Reproduced with permission.

*S*upreme Court ruling aims to give judges and juries an opportunity to consider 'mitigating circumstances' before sentencing a juvenile offender to life in prison, without possibility of parole.

Washington—In a major decision issued Monday, the US Supreme Court struck down mandatory sentencing schemes requiring juvenile defendants to serve life in prison without the possibility of parole.

Voting 5 to 4, the high court declared that automatically sentencing someone so young to a lifetime behind bars—with no future prospect than to die in prison—is cruel and unusual punishment in violation of the Constitution's Eighth Amendment.

"The Eighth Amendment forbids a sentencing scheme that mandates life in prison without the possibility of parole for juvenile offenders," Justice Elena Kagan wrote in the majority decision. "A judge or jury must have the opportunity to consider mitigating circumstances before imposing the harshest possible penalty for juveniles," she said.

Justice Kagan said mandatory sentencing provisions eliminate the ability of a sentencing court to take into consideration all mitigating circumstances about a juvenile's life and involvement in the crime before concluding that life without parole is appropriate punishment for a young offender.

"Although we do not foreclose a sentencer's ability to make that judgment in homicide cases, we require it to take into account how children are different, and how those differences counsel against irrevocably sentencing them to a lifetime in prison," she wrote.

Two justices, Stephen Breyer and Sonia Sotomayor, favored imposing a blanket ban on all life-without-parole sentences for juveniles. While rejecting that option, Kagan noted: "We think appropriate occasions for sentencing juveniles to this harshest possible penalty will be uncommon."

Kagan said juvenile offenders should not be punished as harshly as adults, because they are generally less culpable than adults for their crimes, and enjoy a higher capacity to change. Studies have shown that judgment and character are not fully formed until an individual reaches his or her 20s.

The high court used that same rationale concerning the development of the brain and emotional maturity to justify two other landmark rulings—declaring the death penalty for juvenile offenders unconstitutional in 2005 and deciding in 2010 that sentencing a juvenile to life without parole for a non-homicide crime violated the Eighth Amendment.

The deciding fifth vote in all three cases was cast by the same justice, Anthony Kennedy.

In a dissenting opinion, Chief Justice John Roberts said the Monday decision is not a logical extension of the court's earlier holdings in 2005 and 2010.

"Those cases undoubtedly stand for the proposition that teenagers are less mature, less responsible, and less fixed in their ways than adults—not that a Supreme Court case was needed to establish that," he said.

"What they do not stand for, and do not even suggest, is that legislators—who also know that teenagers are different from adults—may not require life without parole for juveniles who commit the worst types of murder," he said.

"The court's opinion suggests that it is merely a way station on the path to further judicial displacement of the legislative role in prescribing punishment for crime," the chief justice wrote.

"Perhaps science and policy suggest society should show greater mercy to young killers, giving them greater chance to reform themselves at the risk that they will kill again," Roberts said. "But that is not our decision to make."

Currently about 2,500 individuals are serving life without parole prison sentences for crimes committed when they were younger than 18 years old. Of those, roughly 2,000 of the sentences were mandatory.

Thirty-eight states and the federal government allow life-without-parole sentences for juveniles. Twenty-nine states include provisions for mandatory life-without-parole sentences.

Monday's decision stems from two consolidated cases, *Evan Miller v. Alabama* (10-9646) and *Kuntrell Jackson v. Hobbs* (10-9647). Both cases involved murders committed when the boys were 14.

Viewpoint

5

America's Criminal Justice Approach to Juvenile Crimes Is Incoherent

"Many Americans clearly think the kids are not all right. Now if only they could decide who they think 'the kids' are."

A. Barton Hinkle

In the following viewpoint A. Barton Hinkle contends that America is conflicted about how to treat its teenagers. Many state laws regarding the maturity of youth are incoherent, he says. Some states punish juvenile offenders as young as ten as adults but require parental consent before a sixteen- or seventeen-year-old can obtain an abortion. This reflects contradictory presumptions about youth maturity, according to Hinkle. Hinkle is a columnist at the *Richmond Times-Dispatch* in Virginia.

AS YOU READ, CONSIDER THE FOLLOWING QUESTIONS:

1. Why was Sarah Bustamantes arrested, according to Hinkle?
2. At what age does Hinkle say children in Mississippi can be tried as adults for any criminal offense?
3. What two things does Hinkle say are driving incoherent state approaches to youth maturity?

A. Barton Hinkle, "Are Teenagers Big Children or Little Adults?," Reason.com, July 4, 2012. Copyright © 2012 by Richmond Post-Dispatch. All rights reserved. Reproduced with permission.

America can't make up its mind. This should not be surprising in a nation of 314 million people, half of whom can't make up their minds about what to have for dinner. But dinner is inconsequential. How we treat children is not. And when it comes to the treatment of children, society's approach is wildly incoherent.

Last week [June 25, 2012] the Supreme Court ruled, correctly but far from unanimously, that mandatory life sentences without parole for juvenile killers are wrong. That ruling followed another two years ago [in 2010] saying the same thing about crimes other than homicide. Five years before that [in 2005], the Supreme Court ruled against executing juveniles.

These wise rulings build on our growing understanding of the adolescent brain and how long it takes to reach full development. Advances in neuroscience show that in a host of areas from impulse control to thrill-seeking, humans do not reach full maturity until their early 20s. (Some never do.) So executing teenagers for serious crimes is like spanking toddlers for wetting the bed. Yes, they should know better—but there is more to the question than that.

FAST FACT

According to the US Department of Justice, before the 1970s juveniles could only be transferred to adult criminal courts on a court-ordered case-by-case basis. During the 1970s and 1980s, twenty-seven states enacted automatic or prosecutor-controlled transfers to adult criminal courts.

More Arrests for "Misbehavior"

Meanwhile, more and more children are being arrested and charged with criminal offenses for behavior that used to earn them detention—or less. Twelve-year-old Sarah Bustamantes was arrested at Fulmore Middle School in Austin, Texas, a while back because she sprayed perfume on herself after being told, "you smell." According to a study of the Texas educational system, more than 1,000 pupils have been hauled into court for offenses as minor as "making an unreasonable noise." In one instance, a pupil was arrested for throwing a paper airplane.

The US Supreme Court's rulings on punishment for juveniles in the criminal justice system have created an incoherent policy regarding how juvenile crime is approached, the viewpoint author argues.

You might think: Well, that's Texas for you; they're old-school down there. But it's the same story in many parts of the country. The Justice Department says roughly half of all public schools have police officers patrolling the halls. According to an ACLU [American Civil Liberties Union] study, law enforcement is replacing traditional school discipline in Massachusetts' three largest school districts—Boston, Springfield and Worcester—where more arrests are being made for "misbehavior previously handled informally."

Irreconcilable Positions

State officials don't have to agree with the Supreme Court's view of adolescence. But they ought to be able to agree with themselves. Yet in many cases, they do not. Take Texas. Not only does Texas slap kids with criminal charges for classroom antics, it also allows children as young as 14 to be charged as adults for certain felonies. On the other hand, Texas sets the age of consent for sexual activity at 17. This means that, in the Lone Star state's eyes, a 16-year-old is a fully culpable adult if he robs a gas station—but a defenseless child if he loses his virginity.

What's more, Texas also requires both parental notification and consent before a minor can have an abortion. So in the state's eyes, some 14-year-olds who commit crimes have the maturity and judgment of fully grown adults, but no 17-year-old has the maturity and judgment to make a medical decision for herself. Those two positions cannot be reconciled.

Texas isn't alone. Virginia law takes the same two positions. In Mississippi, children as young as 13 can be tried as adults not only for violent felonies but for any criminal offenses whatsoever—and they must be tried as adults for some felonies, including capital crimes. But both parents must agree before a Mississippi girl just shy of her 18th birthday can have an abortion. In Kansas, the discrepancy is even more stark: 17-year-olds must obtain consent from both parents for an abortion, and the age of sexual consent is 16—but children can be charged as adults for any sort of crime starting at age 10.

Some of this incoherence is driven by ideology: Parental-consent laws are as much about hostility to abortion as they are about concern for young women. Some of it is driven by experience: Events such as the 1999 massacre at Columbine High School [in which two students killed one teacher, twelve students, and themselves] have encouraged a get-tough-on-crime approach in the schools.

And after several high-profile suicides such as those of Jamey Rodemeyer [2011] and Phoebe Prince [2010], who were bullied until they couldn't take it any more, it has become apparent that childish behavior still can have horrific consequences. (Hence every state except Montana now has a state anti-bullying law.) The recent harassment [June 2012] of New York bus monitor Karen Klein and a general coarsening of adolescent culture also contribute to public support for tougher discipline. Many Americans clearly think the kids are not all right. Now if only they could decide who they think "the kids" are.

EVALUATING THE AUTHOR'S ARGUMENTS:

What do you think is the primary message A. Barton Hinkle is trying to convey with his viewpoint? Do you think it is to say that state laws are incoherent or that the laws should be changed? Explain.

Chapter 3

How Can Juvenile Crime Be Reduced?

Many ideas on how juvenile crime can be reduced have been debated.

Viewpoint

1

"It's one of the primary reasons why California experienced a stunning 20 percent drop in juvenile arrests in just one year, between 2010 and 2011, according to provocative new research."

Marijuana Decriminalization Law Brings Down Juvenile Arrests in California

Susan Ferriss

In the following viewpoint Susan Ferriss discusses research showing a significant drop in California juvenile arrest rates in the wake of a 2010 law that made possession of small amounts of marijuana an infraction rather than a crime. Before the law's enactment, juveniles caught with less than an ounce of marijuana were arrested and pulled into the juvenile justice system. According to Ferriss, the research suggests that introducing juveniles to the juvenile justice system for simple marijuana possession made it more likely they would commit future crimes. Ferriss is a reporter for the Center for Public Integrity. Previously she was a correspondent for Cox Newspapers and the *Sacramento Bee*. She is also the coauthor of *The Fight in the Fields*, a history of Cesar Chavez and the farmworker movement.

Susan Ferriss, "Marijuana Decriminalization Law Brings Down Juvenile Arrests in California," Center for Public Integrity, November 26, 2012. Reproduced with permission.

AS YOU READ, CONSIDER THE FOLLOWING QUESTIONS:
1. When did the new California pot law go into effect, according to Ferriss?
2. According to the viewpoint, who noted, when signing California's 2010 law, that simple pot possession was already "an infraction in everything but name"?
3. Ferriss reports that drug-related juvenile arrests fell by what percentage between 2010 and 2011?

It's one of the primary reasons why California experienced a stunning 20 percent drop in juvenile arrests in just one year, between 2010 and 2011, according to provocative new research.

The San Francisco–based Center on Juvenile & Criminal Justice (CJCJ) recently released a policy briefing with an analysis of arrest data collected by the California Department of Justice's Criminal Justice Statistics Center. The briefing, "California Youth Crime Plunges to All-Time Low," identifies a new state marijuana decriminalization law that applies to juveniles, not just adults, as the driving force behind the plummeting arrest totals.

After the new pot law went into effect in January 2011, simple marijuana possession arrests of California juveniles fell from 14,991 in 2010 to 5,831 in 2011, a 61 percent difference, the report by CJCJ senior research fellow Mike Males found.

> ## FAST FACT
>
> According to the American Civil Liberties Union, between 2001 and 2010 there were more than 8 million pot arrests in the United States, or one arrest every thirty-seven seconds.

"Arrests for youths for the largest single drug category, marijuana, fell by 9,000 to a level not seen since before the 1980s implementation of the 'war on drugs,'" Males wrote in the report, released in October.

In November, as Males blogged recently, voters in Washington state and Colorado voted to legalize but regulate marijuana use, like alcohol, for people over 21. California's 2010 law did not legalize marijuana, but it officially knocked down "simple" possession of less than one ounce to an infraction from a misdemeanor—and it applies to minors, not just people over 21. Police don't arrest people for infractions; usually, they ticket them. And infractions are punishable not by jail time, but by fines—a $100 fine in California in the case of less than one ounce of pot.

"I think it was pretty courageous not to put an age limit on it," said Males, a longtime researcher on juvenile justice and a former sociology professor at the University of California at Santa Cruz.

Arresting and putting low-level juvenile offenders into the criminal-justice system pulls many kids deeper into trouble rather than turning them around, Males said, a conclusion many law-enforcement experts share.

California's 2010 law still makes it a misdemeanor for anyone over 18 to possess less than an ounce of pot on school grounds, Males noted. For an adult, that's an offense punishable by a $500 fine, ten days in a county jail or both. A minor caught on school grounds with less than an ounce of marijuana is also guilty of a misdemeanor and faces a $150 fine for the first offense, a $500 fine for a second offense and commitment to youth detention for not more than 10 days.

Before the passage of the 2010 law, Californians caught with less than an ounce of pot were arrested by the thousands every year,

California's Proposition 19 to legalize and tax marijuana failed to pass in 2010, but simple possession of less than an ounce of pot was decriminalized, which greatly reduced the number of youth arrested in the state.

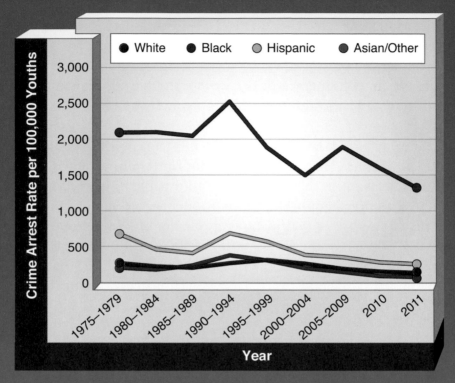

Youth Violent Crime Rate in California by Race, 1975 to 2011

Crime Arrest Rate per 100,000 Youths

- White
- Black
- Hispanic
- Asian/Other

3,000
2,500
2,000
1,500
1,000
500
0

1975–1979 1980–1984 1985–1989 1990–1994 1995–1999 2000–2004 2005–2009 2010 2011

Year

Taken from: Mike Males. "California Crime Rate Plunges To All-Time Low." *Center on Juvenile and Criminal Justice Research Brief*, October 2012.

ultimately facing a fine of $100 . . . and, under certain conditions, referral to drug treatment or education. Many of those arrested were booked, others were released but required to appear in court. They could demand a trial. Strained courts had to take up time ordering diversion treatment programs—a waste of court resources, supporters of a reform said.

Backed by the California District Attorneys Association, the new pot law—passed by state lawmakers—did away with prior requirements that pot offenders be referred to treatment and now allows them to pay a $100 fine akin to that for jaywalking. When Gov. Arnold Schwarzenegger signed the law, he noted that simple pot possession in California was already "an infraction in everything but name."

Males said he suspects that many of the 5,831 marijuana arrests of juveniles in California last year [2011] may have occurred on school grounds. He doesn't have data yet to check his theory, however.

In his police briefing, Males also notes that juvenile arrests in California were the lowest ever recorded since statewide statistics were first compiled in 1954. The decline, Males said, wasn't due just to fewer marijuana arrests.

Drug-related juvenile arrests overall fell by 47 percent between 2010 and 2011. Violent crime arrests fell by 16 percent; homicide arrests by 26 percent; rape arrests by 10 percent; and property-crime arrests by 16 percent. Nationwide, according to the FBI Uniform Crime Reports, arrests of juveniles for all offenses decreased 11.1 percent in 2011 when compared with the 2010 number; arrests of adults declined 3.6 percent.

EVALUATING THE AUTHOR'S ARGUMENTS:

Viewpoint author Susan Ferriss contends that California's marijuana law has led to a reduction in juvenile crime. Name at least one weakness and one strength of her viewpoint.

Viewpoint 2

Marijuana Has Many Dangers, Including a Link to Juvenile Crime

"Legalization of marijuana, no matter how it begins, will come at the expense of our children and public safety."

US Drug Enforcement Agency

The US Drug Enforcement Agency (DEA) is responsible for enforcing federal controlled substance laws and regulations. In the following viewpoint the DEA argues that marijuana is dangerous for many reasons, including that its use leads to juvenile delinquency. According to the DEA, marijuana is associated with students carrying guns to school, fighting, property crimes, and other delinquent behaviors.

AS YOU READ, CONSIDER THE FOLLOWING QUESTIONS:
1. As explained in the viewpoint, what does ONDCP stand for?
2. The report titled *The Relationship between Alcohol, Drug Use, and Violence among Students* was issued by what organization and based on what survey, according to the author?
3. According to the DEA, in 2011 previous month illicit drug use was reported by what percentage of youths who had gotten into a serious fight at school or work?

"The DEA Position on Marijuana," justice.gov, April 2013. United States Department of Justice.

Without a clear understanding of the mental and physical effects of marijuana, its use on our youth, our families, and our society, we will never understand the ramifications it will have on the lives of our younger generation, the impact on their future, and its costs to our society.

Legalization of marijuana, no matter how it begins, will come at the expense of our children and public safety. It will create dependency and treatment issues, and open the door to use of other drugs, impaired health, delinquent behavior, and drugged drivers. . . .

Marijuana use is strongly associated with juvenile crime.

- In a 2008 paper entitled *Non-Medical Marijuana III: Rite of Passage or Russian Roulette*, CASA National Center on Addiction and Substance Abuse reported that in 2006 youth who had been arrested and booked for breaking the law were four times likelier than those who were never arrested to have used marijuana in the past year.

A report titled The Relationship Between Alcohol, Drug Use, and Violence *found that students aged twelve to seventeen who had engaged in fighting or other delinquent behaviors were more likely to have used illicit drugs in the past month.*

- According to CASA in their report on *Criminal Neglect: Substance Abuse, Juvenile Justice and the Children Left Behind,* youth who use marijuana are likelier than those who do not to be arrested and arrested repeatedly. The earlier an individual begins to use marijuana, the likelier he or she is to be arrested.
- Marijuana is known to contribute to delinquent and aggressive behavior. A June 2007 report released by the White House Office of National Drug Control Policy (ONDCP) reveals that teenagers who use drugs are more likely to engage in violent and delinquent behavior. Moreover, early use of marijuana, the most commonly used drug among teens, is a warning sign for later criminal behavior. Specifically, research shows that the instances of physically attacking people, stealing property, and destroying property increase in direct proportion to the frequency with which teens smoke marijuana.

FAST FACT

According to the National Institute on Drug Abuse, estimates from research suggest that about 9 percent of users become addicted to marijuana, and this number increases among those who start young (to about 17 percent, or one in six).

In a report titled *The Relationship between Alcohol, Drug Use, and Violence among Students,* the Community Anti-Drug Coalitions of America (CADCA) reported that according to the 2006 Pride Surveys, during the 2005–2006 school year:

- Of those students who report carrying a gun to school during the 2005–2006 year, 63.9 percent report also using marijuana.
- Of those students who reported hurting others with a weapon at school, 68.4 percent had used marijuana.
- Of those students who reported being hurt by a weapon at school, 60.3 percent reported using marijuana.
- Of those students who reported threatening someone with a gun, knife, or club or threatening to hit, slap or kick someone, 27 percent reported using marijuana.

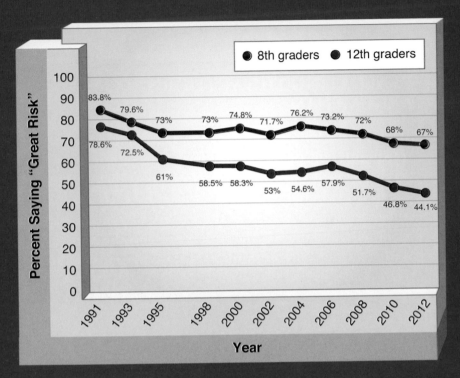

Trends in Perceived Harmfulness of Regular Marijuana Use by Eighth Graders and Twelfth Graders, 1991–2012

8th graders   12th graders

Percent Saying "Great Risk"

83.8%
79.6%
73%   73%   74.8%   76.2%   73.2%   72%
71.7%   68%   67%
78.6%
72.5%
61%
58.5%   58.3%   57.9%
53%   54.6%   51.7%
46.8%   44.1%

Year

Taken from: L.D. Johnston, P.M. O'Malley, J.G. Bachman, and J.E. Schutenberg. *Monitoring the Future National Results on Drug Use: 2012 Overview, Key Findings on Adolescent Drug Use.* Ann Arbor: Institute for Social Research. The University of Michigan, 2013.

- Of those students who reported any trouble with the police, 39 percent also reported using marijuana.
- According to ONDCP, the incidence of youth physically attacking others, stealing, and destroying property increased in proportion to the number of days marijuana was smoked in the past year.
- ONDCP reports that marijuana users were twice as likely as non-users to report they disobeyed school rules.
- Youths aged 12 to 17 who had engaged in fighting or other delinquent behaviors were more likely than other youths to have used illicit drugs in the past month. In 2011 past month illicit drug use was reported by 18.5 percent of youths who had gotten into a

serious fight at school or work compared with 8 percent of those who had not engaged in fighting at school or work, and by 45.1 percent of those who had stolen or tried to steal something worth over $50 in the past year compared with 8.7 percent who had not attempted or engaged in such theft.

EVALUATING THE AUTHOR'S ARGUMENTS:

The US Drug Enforcement Agency (DEA), author of this viewpoint, and the previous viewpoint author, Susan Ferriss, provide various statistics to support their claims. Carefully examine the statistics used by each author, considering such things as the variety of sources, the recentness, and the way the author presents the statistic. Which author do you think uses statistics more effectively, and why?

"The public is safer, youth are being treated less punitively and more humanely, and governments are saving money—because our juvenile justice systems are reducing their reliance on confinement."

Reducing Juvenile Incarceration Leads to Less Juvenile Crime

Annie E. Casey Foundation

In the following viewpoint the Annie E. Casey Foundation (AECF) asserts that a significant decline in youth confinement rates in the United States has made the public safer. According to the AECF, youth incarceration rates in most states started declining in the 1990s. Since then crime rates have fallen significantly. The AECF says that most youth are confined for nonviolent offenses and pose a generally low public safety risk. The AECF is a nonprofit organization dedicated to building better futures for disadvantaged children and their families.

"Reducing Youth Incarceration in the United States," Annie E. Casey Foundation, February 2013. Copyright © 2013 The Annie E. Casey Foundation. All rights reserved. Reproduced with permission.

AS YOU READ, CONSIDER THE FOLLOWING QUESTIONS:

1. In what year did youth confinement peak in the United States, and how many youth were confined on a single day that year, according to data from the US Census Bureau and US Department of Justice provided in this viewpoint?
2. According to the Annie E. Casey Foundation, in 2010 what was the percentage of youth confined due to technical violations of probation, drug possession, low-level property offenses, public order offenses, and status offenses?
3. According to the author, declines in youth confinement rates in individual states have not been driven by national policy, but by what?

A sea change is underway in our nation's approach to dealing with young people who get in trouble with the law. Although we still lead the industrialized world in the rate at which we lock up young people, the youth confinement rate in the United States is rapidly declining. In 2010 this rate reached a new 35-year low, with almost every state confining a smaller share of its youth population than a decade earlier. This decline has not led to a surge in juvenile crime. On the contrary, crime has fallen sharply even as juvenile justice systems have locked up fewer delinquent youth. The public is safer, youth are being treated less punitively and more humanely, and governments are saving money—because our juvenile justice systems are reducing their reliance on confinement. . . .

> **FAST FACT**
>
> America's youth custody rate was 336 out of every 100,000 youths in 2002, nearly five times the rate of the next highest nation, South Africa (69 out of every 100,000 youths), according to data from the London Youth Justice Board.

Wholesale incarceration of young people is generally a counterproductive public policy. As documented in the Annie E. Casey Foundation's 2011 report, *No Place for Kids: The Case for Reducing Juvenile Incarceration,* juvenile corrections facilities are enormously costly to operate, often put youth at risk for injury and abuse and are largely ineffective in reducing recidivism. While youth who have committed serious violent crimes may require incarceration, a large proportion of those currently confined have not been involved in the kinds of serious offending that pose a compelling risk to public safety. The current de-institutionalization trend creates the potential for new, innovative responses to delinquency that are more cost-effective and humane, and lead to better outcomes for youth.

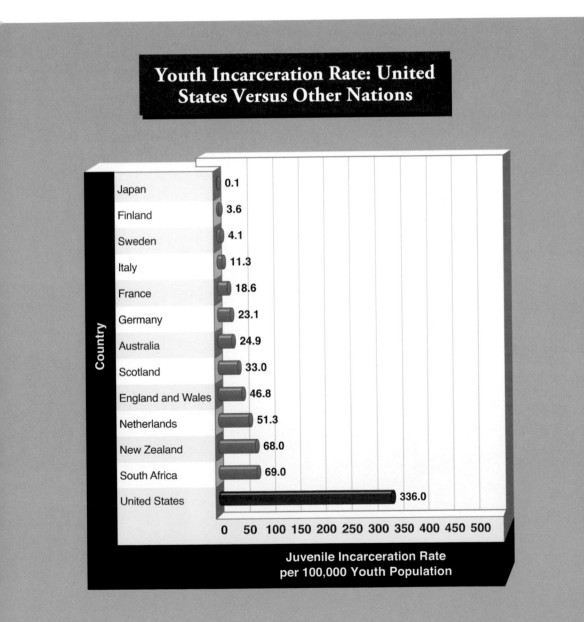

Youth Incarceration Rate: United States Versus Other Nations

Country	Juvenile Incarceration Rate per 100,000 Youth Population
Japan	0.1
Finland	3.6
Sweden	4.1
Italy	11.3
France	18.6
Germany	23.1
Australia	24.9
Scotland	33.0
England and Wales	46.8
Netherlands	51.3
New Zealand	68.0
South Africa	69.0
United States	336.0

Taken from: Annie E. Casey Foundation. "No Place for Kids," 2011. www.aecf.org.

Decline in Youth Confinement

Data from the U.S. Census Bureau and the U.S. Department of Justice Office of Juvenile Justice and Delinquency Prevention show that youth confinement peaked in 1995, at 107,637 in confinement on a single day. Since then the number of youth confined has dropped by nearly 37,000 to 70,792. Over that same period, the rate of youth in confinement dropped by 41 percent, from 381 per 100,000 youth to 225 per 100,000. Moreover, this decline has accelerated in recent years. The annual rate of decline from 2006 to 2010 was roughly three times faster than from 1997 to 2006. Despite this rapid decline, the United States still locks up a larger share of the youth population than any other developed country.

Although the vast majority of confined youth are held in facilities for juveniles, a smaller but substantial number of youth are held in adult correctional facilities. According to the National Prisoner Statistics program and the Annual Survey of Jails, on an average day in 2010, some 7,560 youth under age 18 were held in adult jails, and another 2,295 were in adult prisons. These youth are at elevated risk for physical harm and are more likely to reoffend after release, than youth confined in juvenile facilities.

Statistics show that youth incarcerated in adult facilities are more likely to reoffend after release than are youth placed in juvenile facilities.

In every year for which data are available, the overwhelming majority of confined youth are held for nonviolent offenses. In 2010, only one of every four confined youth was locked up based on a Violent Crime Index offense (homicide, aggravated assault, robbery or sexual assault). At the other end of the spectrum, nearly 40 percent of juvenile commitments and detentions are due to technical violations of probation, drug possession, low-level property offenses, public order offenses and status offenses (activities that would not be crimes for adults, such as possession of alcohol or truancy). This means most confined youth pose relatively low public safety risks.

Declines Occurred Across All Races and in All States

The decline in confinement has occurred across all of the five largest racial groups with the biggest declines occurring among Asian and Pacific Islander and Latino youth. However, large disparities remain in youth confinement rates by race. African-American youth are nearly five times more likely to be confined than their white peers. Latino and American Indian youth are between two and three times more likely to be confined. The disparities in youth confinement rates point to a system that treats youth of color, particularly African Americans and Latinos, more punitively than similar white youth.

The decline in youth confinement over the past decade has occurred in states in every region of the country. In fact, 44 states and the District of Columbia experienced a decline in the rate of young people confined since 1997, and several states cut their confinement rates in half or more. While broad-based, these declines have occurred without the benefit of a widely embraced national policy consensus. Rather, they have been driven by diverse influences and idiosyncratic policy changes within states, often prompted by lawsuits, mounting budget pressures or shifts in leadership. The variety of factors that have led states toward de-incarceration is not surprising given that state juvenile justice policy and practice have varied dramatically for many years. In 2010, a young person in South Dakota (the state with the highest youth confinement rate) was 11 times more likely to be locked up than a young person in Vermont (the state with the lowest youth confinement rate).

Moving Forward

The U.S. juvenile justice system has relied far too heavily on incarceration, for far too long. The recent de-incarceration trend provides a unique opportunity to implement responses to delinquency that are more cost-effective and humane, and that provide better outcomes for youth, their families and communities.

EVALUATING THE AUTHOR'S ARGUMENTS:

What evidence does the Annie E. Casey Foundation provide in this viewpoint to back up its claim that reducing youth incarceration leads to less crime?

Viewpoint 4

Programs Rooted Within the Community Are Effective in Reducing Juvenile Crime

Amruta Ghanekar and Sara Taveras

"To tackle youth crime, we must address the root causes of crime, not the act itself."

In the following viewpoint Amruta Ghanekar and Sara Taveras describe a community-based program to reduce juvenile crime in Philadelphia. The program, called Men in Motion in the Community (MIMIC), partners at-risk juveniles from the inner city with male role models who grew up in the same community. According to Ghanekar and Taveras, MIMIC volunteers can provide something inner-city teens are generally lacking: a positive adult role model. Youth can relate to their mentors and form authentic relationships because they come from the same background. The idea behind MIMIC is to show troubled teens that there are

Amruta Ghanekar and Sara Taveras,"MIMIC: Tackling the Root Causes of Juvenile Delinquency," *Philadelphia Social Innovations Journal*, February 2010. Copyright © 2010 by Philadelphia Social Innovations Journal 2010. All rights reserved. Reproduced with permission.

positive options to violence and crime, say the authors. Ghanekar and Taveras are contributors to the *Philadelphia Social Innovations Journal,* a publication that highlights innovative ideas to promote social change.

AS YOU READ, CONSIDER THE FOLLOWING QUESTIONS:
1. According to the authors, what is MIMIC's ultimate goal?
2. In the viewpoint, who says, "These kids are smart and when they realize that we function without any resources other than our passion towards this cause, they develop respect for MIMIC?"
3. According to the authors, MIMIC is an intentional play on words, where the men ask the kids to do what?

T he interconnected issues of violence, poverty, lack of social support, and high school dropout rates have led to an ever-increasing incarceration of young people from inner-city areas with large minority populations. The police, court, and state-run juvenile justice systems' response to social problems is reactive, funneling young people into expensive treatment and reintegration programs. These programs generally have very limited success.

Men in Motion in the Community

Men in Motion in the Community (MIMIC) is a group of men—most of whom are ex-offenders—whose concerns about the high number of youth entering the juvenile justice system prompted them to provide mentorship and crisis intervention to most-at-risk young males (ages 12–17) in their North Philadelphia community. Many of these youth are very hard to reach via conventional channels (like the state-run programs). Given their personal experiences, MIMIC volunteers are able to connect to the youth quickly, eliminating the barriers faced by traditional service providers in engaging extremely at-risk youth. MIMIC offers a proactive, community-based solution that focuses on root causes to prevent youth from entering the juvenile justice system in the first place. In addition, some of the men who volunteer with MIMIC find that transforming their own past prison experiences into a positive contribution to their communities facilitates a more sustainable re-entry experience for them.

To tackle youth crime, we must address the root causes of crime, not the act itself. MIMIC demonstrates that the best way to "reform" the juvenile justice system is to make sure the juveniles don't enter the system at all. The authentic relationships, emphasis on male role models rooted in the community, and similarities in background between MIMIC volunteers and at-risk youth all contribute to the volunteers' success. . . .

MIMIC is focused on helping young men to engage/re-engage in education and strengthen the social networks needed to live a life free of crime and violence. The MIMIC volunteers who grew up in the same locality realize that their lives could have been much different if somebody had shown them options beyond the violence and poverty all around them. They want the young men in Philadelphia's 24th, 25th, and 26th Police Districts to understand that they can have a bright future if they really want it. MIMIC's ultimate goal is to reduce the number of young males of color entering gangs and/or the criminal justice system.

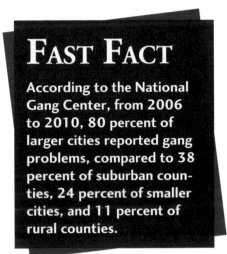

FAST FACT

According to the National Gang Center, from 2006 to 2010, 80 percent of larger cities reported gang problems, compared to 38 percent of suburban counties, 24 percent of smaller cities, and 11 percent of rural counties.

The most innovative components of MIMIC's model include:

- *Relationship*: MIMIC is composed of men with similar backgrounds and cultures who can connect with kids on a personal level.
- *Volunteer model*: The volunteer-driven model conveys MIMIC's authenticity to the kids.
- *Client-centric*: Kids select their own level of involvement with MIMIC and get very personalized attention; MIMIC meets the kids where they are—in school or on the corner—and provides a 24-hour hotline for around-the-clock support.
- *Redemption*: Many MIMIC volunteers have gone through the justice system and are uniquely prepared to work on prevention; MIMIC provides ex-offenders with a sustainable re-entry/re-integration program.

Visiting a prison can help deter youth from criminal activity, but community-based programs that provide good role models are effective as well, contend the authors.

Relationship

The *who* of the MIMIC relationship is what makes such a profound difference. The MIMIC volunteers identify with the young people and earn their trust because they share similarities in culture, language, and background. MIMIC volunteers also have respect in the streets of their communities, which allows for greater mutual respect between the kids and their mentors. Hence, they are equipped to offer the youth what they lack most—a meaningful relationship with a supportive male role model.

Crime committed by juveniles in Philadelphia is partly due to dysfunctional family situations. Most young men do not have a male mentor to look up to and talk to at their most vulnerable and impressionable age. MIMIC volunteers try to solve this problem by offering an intense mentoring relationship. The similar backgrounds, culture, class, and geography help the boys feel comfortable in opening up, and this leads to the formation of an authentic relationship.

Volunteer Model

MIMIC acts as a transformative force leveraging volunteers to effect positive change in their communities. The volunteer force is important because the young people understand that their mentors are driven by internal motives, not financial motives. All the MIMIC volunteers have jobs; they find time for MIMIC before and after work, during holidays, or by using vacation or sick leave time. When the young men see that these mentors are working voluntarily for their betterment, it becomes easier for them to trust MIMIC.

MIMIC was not designed by a group of people outside of the community with a larger agenda. Rather, it evolved naturally as a result of the efforts of a group of responsible men trying to improve the lives of young men in their community. Edwin Desamour, MIMIC's founder, says, "These kids are smart and when they realize that we function without any resources other than our passion towards this cause, they develop respect for MIMIC." It is this trust and respect that helps MIMIC touch the hardest-to-reach young males and win their confidence.

Client-Centric

Typically in existing preventive services, a prescribed service strategy tries to fit young people into one model. However, the relationship that is formed between MIMIC volunteers and the youth is one that responds in a timely fashion to the needs of the young person and is client-centric.

MIMIC can also be distinguished from the state-run juvenile correction programs based on its approach towards the connection. By distributing their hotline numbers, MIMIC volunteers give the kids an option to take the first step; the relationship is initiated by the youth who call. This initiative can play an important role in making them feel responsible for maintaining the relationship, as it is something they have done of their own choice rather than obligation.

Redemption

In the Alcoholics Anonymous model, the best way to stay sober is to help another alcoholic. In this same way, MIMIC reinforces its mission on two fronts: preventing youth from entering the justice system helps MIMIC volunteers from re-entering the system.

MIMIC volunteers struggle with their own histories of abusive childhoods, addiction, violence, or poverty. The name MIMIC is an intentional play on words—the men ask the kids to mimic them and not the drug dealers running the streets. Through the opportunity to turn their lives around, MIMIC is helping its volunteers stay focused and giving them a reason to act responsibly: they love these kids, and these kids look up to them. Oftentimes after making a presentation, a MIMIC volunteer will say, "I really needed that." This response reinforces the authenticity of the mentoring relationships; they need the kids just as much as the kids need them.

In addition, the structure of MIMIC provides the adult male volunteers with a social support network among themselves. The men work out together as a way to vent their stress, and check in with each other regularly. Occasionally, after meetings, which are routinely held in churches and community centers, the men end with a prayer, and some help out with ministries at the churches. Some volunteers cite MIMIC as a way to work through the guilt they carry. For many of them, preventing other youth from entering the system is the path to confession, forgiveness, and redemption.

EVALUATING THE AUTHOR'S ARGUMENTS:

Do you think viewpoint authors Amruta Ghanekar and Sara Taveras do a good job of explaining why a community-based approach is more effective than other approaches to reduce juvenile crime? Why or why not? Provide specific examples from the text when explaining your answer.

Scared Straight Programs Are Not Effective

Laurie O. Robinson and Jeff Slowikowski

"'Scared straight' is not only ineffective but is potentially harmful. And it may run counter to the law."

In the following viewpoint Laurie O. Robinson and Jeff Slowikowski contend that scared straight programs are ineffective at best and harmful at worst. According to Robinson and Slowikowski, researchers have studied the impacts of scared straight programs and found that participating teens were more likely rather than less likely to become involved in crime afterward. Robinson and Slowikowski say that the federal government has recognized the potential harm of scared straight programs and will no longer fund them. States are encouraged to adopt other approaches to reduce juvenile crime, such as mentoring programs, they say. Robinson is a US Department of Justice assistant attorney general, and Slowikowski is the acting administrator for the Justice Department's Office of Juvenile Justice and Delinquency Prevention.

Laurie O. Robinson and Jeff Slowikowski, "Scary—and Ineffective," *Baltimore Sun*, October 11, 2013. Reproduced with permission.

AS YOU READ, CONSIDER THE FOLLOWING QUESTIONS:
  1. According to the authors, what percentage of participants in scared straight programs did researchers find were more likely to reoffend?
  2. According to Robinson and Slowikowski, what provides the juvenile justice field with the best tool for sound decision making?
  3. How long has the Department of Justice supported mentoring programs, as stated in the viewpoint?

"Scared straight" programs have long been wildly popular in this country as a get-tough response to juvenile crime. They typically involve bringing at-risk youths into an adult prison, where they are confronted—in shocking and brutal fashion—by adult inmates. These programs may include tours of the facility and personal stories from prisoners and may even integrate the youths into the prison population for up to a day. Experiencing the harsh reality of life behind bars is thought to deter kids from a life of crime by frightening them into changing their behavior.

The A&E Network is currently airing "Beyond Scared Straight," a series highlighting four of these programs across the country. A recent episode followed five youths who were brought to the Maryland Correctional Institution at Jessup, which houses more than 1,000 inmates. These youths came face to face with what the A&E website described as "menacing inmates, including convicted murderers, [who] surround the kids and taunt them." The network portrays such programs as effective in keeping youths from becoming lifelong criminals.

> ## FAST FACT
>
> The original scared straight program began in the 1970s at New Jersey's Rahway State Prison. It was the focus of a television special in 1978.

Scared Straight Programs Are Harmful

Unfortunately, the research tells us otherwise: "scared straight" is not only ineffective but is potentially harmful. And it may run counter to the law.

Anthony Petrosino and a team of researchers from the Campbell Collaboration, an international research network, analyzed the findings from evaluations of nine scared straight–type programs. In contrast to the claims of proponents, Mr. Petrosino and his colleagues found that these programs did not deter teenage participants from offending; in fact, they were *more* likely to offend in the future. Across the evaluated programs, participants were up to 28 percent more likely to offend than youths who didn't participate. To add insult to injury, a number of youths reported to evaluators that adult inmates sexually propositioned them and tried to steal their belongings. Not only was scared straight found not to deter criminal behavior, the study strongly suggested the program caused harm. The fact that these types of programs are still being touted as effective, despite stark evidence to the contrary, is troubling. In the decades following the original scared straight program, states across the country developed similar models in the hopes that this get-tough approach would make an impact on their impressionable youth. As it turns out, the impact was not the one they had hoped for.

Fortunately, in recent years, policymakers and criminal and juvenile justice practitioners have begun to recognize that answers about what works are best found in sound research, not in storytelling. Evidence

Comparing the Costs and Benefits of Programs to Reduce Juvenile Crime in Washington State, 2012

Juvenile Program	Cost*	Long-Term Benefits	Cost/Benefit Ratio
Functional Family Therapy	$3,262	$70,370	$21.57
Aggression-replacement training	$1,508	$62,947	$41.75
Coordination of services	$395	$5,501	$13.94
Scared straight	$65	-$4,949	-$76.35

*Washington State, 2012 dollars.

Taken from: Gary Vanlandingham. "Evidence-Based Policy Making, The Shape of Things to Come." Pew-MacArthur Results First Initiative, August 22, 2013.

Some studies have found that so-called scared straight programs do not deter teenage participants from offending; in fact, some participants were seen to be more likely to offend in the future.

from science provides the field with the best tool for sound decision-making. This "smart on crime" approach saves taxpayer money and maximizes limited government resources—especially critical at a time of budget cuts.

In light of this evidence, the U.S. Department of Justice discourages the funding of scared straight–type programs. States that operate such programs could have their federal funding reduced if shown not to have complied with the Juvenile Justice and Delinquency Prevention Act.

Programs That Work

So what does research tell us about what *does* work? Mentoring programs have been found to be effective in reducing incidents of delinquency, substance use and academic failure in participating youth. Mentoring is a process that uses positive relationships to teach, impart or institute changes in a youth's behavior or attitudes. Research has shown that mentoring relationships that last at least 12 months or through an entire school year are most effective. Further, youth in long-term mentoring relationships tend to improve their self-esteem, social skills and outlook about their future.

The Department of Justice has supported mentoring programs for more than 30 years as a primary prevention tool to address juvenile delinquency. Not surprisingly, research suggests that offering at-risk youth a relationship with a positive role model has more benefit than scaring them with a negative one.

It is understandable why desperate parents hoping to divert their troubled children from further misbehavior would place their hopes in a program they see touted as effective on TV, and why in years past policymakers opted to fund what appeared to be an easy fix for juvenile offending. However, we have a responsibility—as both policymakers and parents—to follow evidence, not anecdote, in finding answers, especially when it comes to our children.

EVALUATING THE AUTHOR'S ARGUMENTS:

The authors of this viewpoint, Laurie O. Robinson and Jeff Slowikowski, believe that mentoring is preferable to scared straight programs in deterring youth from a lifetime of crime. As explained by the authors, how do the two programs differ in approach and outcomes?

Facts About Juvenile Crime

Editor's note: These facts can be used in reports to add credibility when making important points or claims.

According to the Centers for Disease Control and Prevention (CDC):

- In 2010, 4,828 young people ages 10 to 24 were victims of homicide—an average of thirteen each day.
- Homicide is the second leading cause of death for young people ages 15 to 24.
- Among homicide victims ages 10 to 24 in 2010, 86 percent (4,171) were male and 14 percent (657) female.
- Among homicide victims ages 10 to 24 in 2010, 82.8 percent were killed with a firearm.
- Among 10- to 24-year-olds, homicide is the leading cause of death for African Americans; the second leading cause of death for Hispanics; and the third leading cause of death for American Indians and Alaska Natives.
- During the 2009–2010 school year, seventeen homicides of youth ages 5 to 18 occurred at school.
- Approximately 1 percent of all youth homicides in 2008–2009 occurred at school, and the rate of all youth homicides occurring at school has been less than 2 percent since the 1992–1993 school year.
- There was approximately one homicide or suicide of a school-age youth at school per 2.7 million students enrolled during the 2009–2010 school year.
- Each year, youth homicides and assault-related injuries result in an estimated $16 billion in combined medical and work-loss costs.

According to the CDC, in a 2011 nationally representative sample of youth in grades nine to twelve:

- 32.8 percent reported being in a physical fight in the 12 months preceding the survey.

- 16.6 percent reported carrying a weapon (gun, knife, or club) on 1 or more days in the 30 days preceding the survey.
- 5.1 percent reported carrying a gun on 1 or more days in the 30 days preceding the survey.
- 5.4 percent reported carrying a weapon (gun, knife, or club) on school property on 1 or more days in the 30 days preceding the survey.
- 7.4 percent reported being threatened or injured with a weapon on school property one or more times in the 12 months preceding the survey.
- 20.1 percent reported being bullied on school property in the 12 months preceding the survey.
- 16.2 percent reported being bullied electronically (e-mail, chat room, website, texting) in the 12 months preceding the survey.

Facts About Juvenile Arrests

According to the latest data available from the US Department of Justice, in 2010:

- Law enforcement agencies in the United States made 1.6 million arrests of persons under age eighteen in 2010, including
    - 1,000 arrests for murder and nonnegligent manslaughter,
    - 2,900 arrests for forcible rape,
    - 72,000 arrests for robbery and aggravated assault,
    - 366,600 property crimes, and
    - 170,600 drug abuse violations.

- Of all juvenile arrests for violent crimes in 2010,
    - 47 percent involved white youth,
    - 51 percent involved black youth,
    - 1 percent involved Asian youth, and
    - 1 percent involved American Indian youth.

- The number of arrests of juveniles in 2010 was 21 percent fewer than the number of arrests in 2001.
- In 2010 law enforcement made 480,000 arrests of females younger than age eighteen.
- In 2010 females accounted for 18 percent of juvenile arrests for violent crimes (murder, rape, robbery, and aggravated assault),

38 percent of juvenile property crime arrests, and 45 percent of juvenile larceny-theft arrests.

- Youth younger than age fifteen accounted for more than one-fourth of all juvenile arrests for violent and property crimes.
- Forty percent of all persons arrested for arson in 2010 were younger than age eighteen; 1 in 4 were younger than age fifteen.
- The juvenile arrest rate for simple assault in 2010 was more than twice the 1980 rate.
- The juvenile arrest rate for burglary, property crimes, and aggravated assault in 2010 was at its lowest since at least 1980.
- The juvenile arrest rate for forcible rape in 2010 was one-third its 1991 peak.
- In 2010 juveniles were involved in about 1 in 10 arrests for murder; about 1 in 4 arrests for robbery, burglary, and disorderly conduct; and about 1 in 5 arrests for larceny-theft and motor vehicle theft.

Facts About Juvenile Lifers

- According to the Center for Children's Law and Policy, in 2014 in the United States, more than twenty-five hundred individuals were behind bars for life without the possibility of parole for crimes that they committed as juveniles.
- According to a national survey conducted by the Sentencing Project and published in March 2012:
  - Seventy-nine percent of individuals reported witnessing violence in their homes.
  - More than half (54.1 percent) witnessed weekly violence in their neighborhoods.
  - Nearly half (46.9 percent) experienced physical abuse, including 79.5 percent of girls.
  - 77.3 percent of girls reported histories of sexual abuse; overall, 20.5 percent of juvenile lifers report being victims of sexual abuse.
  - A third (31.5 percent) of juvenile lifers were raised in public housing.
  - 17.9 percent of the respondents were not living with a close adult relative just before their incarceration; some reported

being homeless, living with friends, or being housed in a detention facility, treatment center, or group home.

- Two in five respondents had been enrolled in special education classes.
- Fewer than half (46.6 percent) were attending school at the time of their offense.
- 84.4 percent had been suspended or expelled from school at some point in their academic career.
- The proportion of African Americans serving a life sentence who were sentenced as youths for the killing of a white person (43.4 percent) is nearly twice the rate at which African American juveniles are arrested for taking a black person's life (23.2 percent).

Facts About State Juvenile Justice Laws

According to the Campaign for Youth Justice, between 2011 and 2013:

- Eleven states (Colorado, Hawaii, Idaho, Indiana, Maine, Nevada, Ohio, Oregon, Pennsylvania, Texas, and Virginia) passed laws limiting states' authority to house youth in adult jails and prisons.
- Four states (Connecticut, Illinois, Massachusetts, and Mississippi) expanded their juvenile court jurisdiction so that older youths who previously would be automatically tried as adults are no longer prosecuted in adult criminal court.
- Eleven states (Arizona, Colorado, Connecticut, Delaware, Illinois, Maryland, Nevada, Ohio, Utah, Virginia, and Washington) changed their transfer laws, making it more likely that youth will stay in the juvenile justice system.

Organizations to Contact

The editors have compiled the following list of organizations concerned with the issues debated in this book. The descriptions are derived from materials provided by the organizations. All have publications or information available for interested readers. The list was compiled on the date of publication of the present volume; the information provided here may change. Be aware that many organizations take several weeks or longer to respond to inquiries, so allow as much time as possible for the receipt of requested materials.

Campaign for Youth Justice (CFYJ)
1220 L St. NW, Ste. 605
Washington, DC 20005
(202) 558-3580
fax: (202) 386-9807
e-mail: info@cfyj.org
website: www.campaignforyouthjustice.org

The CFYJ is a nonprofit organization dedicated to ending the practice of trying, sentencing, and incarcerating youth under age eighteen in the adult criminal justice system. The campaign works in partnership with state-based campaigns in a number of states and serves as a clearinghouse of information on youth prosecuted as adults. The CFYJ produces fact sheets and reports about state juvenile justice laws, such as *State Trends: Legislative Victories 2011–2013*.

Center for Children's Law and Policy (CCLP)
1701 K St. NW, Ste. 1100
Washington, DC 20006
(202) 637-0377
fax: (202) 379-1600
e-mail: info@cclp.org
website: http://www.cclp.org

The CCLP is a public interest law and policy organization focused on reform of juvenile justice and other systems that affect troubled and at-risk children, as well as protection of the rights of children in those systems. The center's work covers a range of activities, including research, writing, public education, media advocacy, training, technical assistance, administrative and legislative advocacy, and litigation. The CCLP produces various publications and a monthly e-newsletter, the *DMC e-News*.

Center for the Study and Prevention of Violence (CSPV)
Institute of Behavioral Science
University of Colorado–Boulder, 483 UCB
Boulder, CO 80309-0483
(303) 492-1032
fax: (303) 492-2151
e-mail: cspv@colorado.edu
website: www.colorado.edu/cspv

The CSPV provides assistance to groups committed to understanding and preventing violence, particularly adolescent violence. It achieves this mission by disseminating information to the public, offering technical assistance to those working in violence prevention, and conducting basic research into the causes of violence and the effectiveness of violence prevention programs. Safe Communities Safe Schools is a project of the CSPV that assists schools with violence prevention planning, evidence-based programming, training, and technical assistance, as well as prevention and safety research resources. The CSPV produces numerous publications available on its website.

Center on Juvenile and Criminal Justice (CJCJ)
40 Boardman Pl.
San Francisco, CA 94103
(415) 621-5661
fax: (415) 621-5466
e-mail: cjcjmedia@cjcj.org
website: www.cjcj.org

The CJCJ is a nonprofit organization whose mission is to reduce society's reliance on incarceration as a solution to social problems. In pursuit of this mission, the CJCJ provides direct services, technical assistance, and policy analysis in order to promote a balanced and humane criminal justice system designed to reduce incarceration and enhance long-term public safety. The CJCJ publishes the *Justice Policy Journal* as well as a monthly newsletter and a blog.

Family Violence Prevention Fund (FVPF)
383 Rhode Island St., Ste. 304
San Francisco, CA 94103
(415) 252-8900
fax: (415) 252-8991
e-mail: info@endabuse.org
website: www.endabuse.org

The FVPF believes everyone has a right to a life without violence. The organization works to end violence against women and children around the world and to help those who have been victims of violence. The FVPF promotes violence-prevention efforts and educates health-care providers, police, judges, employers, and others about ways to address violence. The organization offers many materials on its website about children and domestic violence.

Johns Hopkins Center for the Prevention of Youth Violence (JHCPYV)
Johns Hopkins Bloomberg School of Public Health
624 N. Broadway, Rm. 819
Baltimore, MD 21205
(410) 955-3962
fax: (410) 955-9088
e-mail: pleaf@jhsph.edu
website: www.jhsph.edu

The JHCPYV is one of six Centers of Excellence in Youth Violence Prevention funded by the Centers for Disease Control and Prevention. The goals of the JHCPYV is to create, implement, and evaluate a multifaceted, evidence-based approach to youth violence prevention in a high-risk Baltimore community; and integrate training activities for early career researchers, educators, practitioners, community residents, and youth in youth violence prevention. The center provides a compilation of resources and links to websites containing useful information on the prevention of youth violence as well as positive youth development.

National Center for Children Exposed to Violence (NCCEV)
Yale University
Child Study Center
230 South Frontage Rd.
New Haven, CT 06520
(877) 496-2238
fax: (203) 785-4608
website: www.nccev.org

The mission of the NCCEV is to help individuals and communities reduce the incidence and impact of violence on children and families, train and support the professionals who provide intervention and treatment to children and families affected by violence, and increase professional and public awareness of the effects of violence on children, families, communities, and society. The NCCEV Resource Center provides public access to a wide variety of materials on children's exposure to violence within homes, schools, and communities.

National Center for Mental Health and Juvenile Justice (NCMHJJ)
Policy Research Associates
345 Delaware Ave.
Delmar, NY 12054
(866) 962-6455
e-mail: ncmhjj@prainc.com
website: www.ncmhjj.com

The mission of the NCMHJJ is to help improve policies and programs for youth with mental health disorders in contact with the juvenile justice system. The center collects, develops, and disseminates information and resources on youth with behavioral health needs in contact with the juvenile justice system; influences practice to bring about improved services for youth through training and technical assistance; and informs and improves public policy at the national, state, and local levels that reflects the best available research and practice. The NCMHJJ offers numerous resources on a variety of topics, including mental health screening in juvenile justice settings and implementing evidence-based practices.

National Center for Victims of Crime (NCVC)
2000 M St. NW, Ste. 480
Washington, DC 20036

(202) 467-8700
fax: (202) 467-8701
e-mail: webmaster@ncvc.org
website: www.ncvc.org

The NCVC is the nation's leading resource and advocacy organization for crime victims and those who serve them. The center works with grassroots organizations and criminal justice agencies throughout the United States to serve millions of crime victims. The NCVC website provides many of the organization's reports and studies, such as *Snitches Get Stitches, Teen Action Toolkit*, and *Our Vulnerable Teenagers.*

National Organization of Victims of Juvenile Lifers (NOVJL)
PO Box 498
Davisburg, MI 48350-0498
(248) 736-1737
e-mail: NOVJL@aol.com
website: www.teenkillers.org

The NOVJL supports and informs victims of juveniles serving life sentences and advocates for victims' rights in the criminal justice system. The organization believes victims' voices must be heard in the public policy debate about the complicated matter of juvenile justice for teens who kill. The NOVJL supports the availability of a wide range of sentencing options for the courts to use when looking at the individual facts of each offense and determining the best punishment and the best outcome for public safety. The NOVJL website provides victim memorials, myths and facts, and news about juveniles who murder.

Office of Juvenile Justice and Delinquency Prevention (OJJDP)
810 Seventh St. NW
Washington, DC 20531
(202) 307-5911
e-mail: http://askjj.ncjrs.gov
website: www.ojjdp.gov

The OJJDP seeks to meet the challenge of juveniles in crisis—from serious, violent, and chronic offenders to victims of abuse and neglect. It supports states, local communities, and tribal jurisdictions in their efforts to develop and implement effective programs for juveniles. The OJJDP sponsors research, program, and training initiatives; develops priorities and goals and sets policies to guide federal juvenile justice issues; disseminates information about juvenile justice issues; and awards funds to states to support local programming. The OJJDP produces numerous publications, including the *Journal of Juvenile Justice.*

For Further Reading

Books

Bernard, Thomas J., and Megan C. Kurlychek. *The Cycle of Juvenile Justice*. New York: Oxford University Press, 2010. The authors examine the history of juvenile justice policies in the United States. Going back more than two hundred years, the book reveals that policies cycle between lenient treatment and harsh punishments for juvenile delinquents.

Cornell, Dewey. *School Violence: Fears Versus Facts*. New York: Routledge, 2006. Forensic psychologist Dewey Cornell uses case studies to identify myths and misconceptions about youth violence, from bullying to rampage shootings. According to Cornell, fear of school violence has resulted in misguided, counterproductive educational policies and practices ranging from boot camps to zero tolerance.

Elrod, Preston, and R. Scott Ryder. *Juvenile Justice: A Social, Historical and Legal Perspective*. Sudbury, MA: Jones & Bartlett Learning, 2009. The authors provide a comprehensive look at the multifaceted juvenile justice system in the United States, one that is constantly changing because of policies and laws. By examining the history, theory, and components of the juvenile justice system, the authors hope to make it more understandable.

Hubner, John. *Last Chance in Texas: The Redemption of Criminal Youth*. New York: Random House, 2008. Hubner follows two youths incarcerated at Giddings State School in Texas. Giddings is home to teenagers convicted of the most violent crimes in Texas; yet surprisingly, the school has success in rehabilitating the youths who come through its doors. Hubner chronicles the two youths, one female and one male, as they participate in group therapy sessions and recount their crimes and the abuse they suffered as children.

Humes, Edward. *No Matter How Loud I Shout: A Year in the Life of Juvenile Court*. New York: Simon & Schuster, 1997. Pulitzer prize–

winning author Humes depicts the lives of seven young people caught up in the California juvenile justice system in 1994. He also describes the efforts of the judges, deputies, probation officers, and public defenders who cope with and try to help the juveniles entering the system.

Kotlowitz, Alex. *There Are No Children Here: The Story of Two Boys Growing Up in the Other America*. New York: Doubleday, 1992. This book chronicles the true story of two young brothers living in a violence-ridden public housing project in Chicago in the 1990s. The brothers are confronted with violent gangs, persistent poverty, and personal tragedies, yet find a way to survive. The author illustrates what life in the inner-city ghetto is like for young children and the overwhelming odds they must overcome to break out of the vicious cycle of poverty and crime.

Kunerth, Jeff. *Trout: A True Story of Murder, Teens, and the Death Penalty*. Gainesville: University Press of Florida, 2012. Kunerth, a reporter for the *Orlando Sentinel*, details the true story of a murder-for-hire plot at the Trout Auto Parts store in Pensacola, Florida, in 1991 that resulted in the death of an unintended victim and put three teens on death row. The author reveals what it is like to be a young person with few opportunities whose life changes in a matter of minutes. He also makes a strong argument against sentencing juveniles as adults.

Kutner, Lawrence, and Cheryl Olson. *Grand Theft Childhood*. New York: Simon & Schuster, 2008. Kutner and Olson, husband and wife founders of the Harvard Medical School Center for Mental Health and Media, examine whether video games are responsible for a rise in social violence. The authors find some surprising results and provide evenhanded information on violence and video games.

Monahan, Torin, and Rodolfo D. Torees, eds. *Schools Under Surveillance: Cultures of Control in Public Education*. New Brunswick, NJ: Rutgers University Press, 2009. This book is a compilation of essays addressing surveillance and discipline in public schools. Contributing authors discuss police and military recruiters on campus, testing and accountability regimes such as No Child Left Behind, and efforts by students and teachers to circumvent the most egregious forms of surveillance in public education.

Myers, David L. *Boys Among Men: Trying and Sentencing Juveniles as Adults.* Westport, CT: Praeger, 2005. Myers examines America's treatment of juvenile delinquents as adult criminals. He examines the demographic, legal, criminal, and social characteristics of those youth who are waived to adult courts, assessing the nature, use, and effectiveness of punishment and rehabilitation efforts in modern juvenile and criminal justice systems.

Rios, Victor M. *Punished: Policing the Lives of Black and Latino Boys.* New York: New York University Press, 2011. In this book, Rios, a former gang member who went on to earn a PhD, details the coming-of-age stories of young men of color in his old Oakland, California, neighborhood. According to Rios, these young men face poverty, violence, and institutionalized racism. They are labeled as dangerous or difficult starting in grade school and face harsh punishment for petty violations, which the author says pushes young men into the very criminality that the punishment is meant to deter.

Schaffner, Laurie. *Girls in Trouble with the Law.* New Brunswick, NJ: Rutgers University Press, 2006. Sociologist Schaffner goes inside juvenile detention centers to explore the lives of incarcerated adolescent and teen girls. Most of these young women are girls of color who report having experienced physical harm and sexual assaults.

Venkatesh, Sudhir. *Gang Leader for a Day: A Rogue Sociologist Takes to the Streets.* New York: Penguin, 2008. This book is a result of first-year graduate student Venkatesh's friendship with a Chicago gang leader named JT. Under JT's protection, Venkatesh got an inside look at life in an urban war zone.

Ward, Geoff K. *The Black Child-Savers: Racial Democracy and Juvenile Justice.* Chicago: University of Chicago Press, 2012. Ward presents a study of what he calls a Jim Crow juvenile justice system in the United States. He examines the origins and organization of a separate and unequal juvenile justice system and explores how generations of "black child-savers" arose to overcome the threat to black youths.

Periodicals and Internet Sources

Booth, Brandi, Vincent B. Van Hasselt, and Gregory M. Vecchi. "Addressing School Violence," *FBI Law Enforcement Bulletin*, May

2011. www.fbi.gov/stats-services/publications/law-enforcement
-bulletin/may_2011/school_violence.

Christian Science Monitor. "America Corrects a Mistake: Trying
Minors as Adults," March 7, 2011.

Drum, Kevin. "Race, Lead, and Juvenile Crime," *Mother Jones*,
August 16, 2013. www.motherjones.com/kevin-drum/2013/08
/lead-crime-racism-black-white-juvenile.

Ferriss, Susan. "Throwaway Kids: Disciplined California Teens
Struggle to School Themselves," Center for Public Integrity, July
15, 2013. www.publicintegrity.org/2013/07/15/12951/throw
away-kids-disciplined-california-teens-struggle-school-themselves.

Fragassi, Joe. "31 School Shootings in America Since Columbine, Only
14 in the Rest of the World Combined," PolicyMic, December 15,
2012. www.policymic.com/articles/20843/31-school-shootings-in
-america-since-columbine-only-14-in-the-rest-of-the-world
-combined.

Goeld, Rashmi. "Delinquent or Distracted? Attention Deficit Disorder
and the Construction of the Juvenile Offender," *Law & Inequality:
A Journal of Theory and Practice*, Winter 2009.

Herbert, Wray. "Is Juvenile Delinquency a Failure of Imagination?,"
Huffington Post, October 3, 2012. www.huffingtonpost.com/wray
-herbert/is-juvenile-delinquency-a_b_1937273.html.

Howe, Sam, and Charisma L. Miller. "When Should We Hold Parents
Legally Responsible for Heinous Acts of Children?," *Brooklyn Daily
Eagle*, December 17, 2012.

Hunt, Angie. "Teen's Criminal Career Can Start by Age 5," Futurity,
January 30, 2013. www.futurity.org/teens-criminal-career-can
-start-by-age-5.

Keilman, John. "20 Years After Winnetka Murder, Women Remain
Inspired by Sister's Dying Statement," *Chicago Tribune*, April 7,
2010.

King, Colbert I. "When Fatherless Young Offenders Are Fathers
Themselves," *Washington Post*, December 21, 2012.

Kirchner, Lauren. "Treating Mental Illness Prevents Crime and Saves
Us Money," *Pacific Standard*, June 14, 2013. www.psmag.com

Index

Supreme Court bars mandatory life sentences for, 63–67

Nossel, Suzanne, 66

O
Obama, Barack, 9, 40
Office of National Drug Control
    Policy (ONDCP), 80, 81
Opinion polls. *See* Surveys

P
Parents, influence of violent
    video games need to be
    understood by, 15–16
Parker, Courtney, 33
Petrosino, Anthony, 97
PolicyMic.com (website), 34
Polls. *See* Surveys
Post-traumatic stress disorder
    (PTSD), 25
Prevention
    community programs are
        effective in, 89–94
    parents' role in, 15–16
    of school shootings, 42–43
    of school violence, 36–38
    through mentoring programs,
        98–99
Prince, Phoebe, 71
Psychology Today (magazine), 19
PTSD (post-traumatic stress
    disorder), 25

R
Race/ethnicity
    California youth violent crime
        rate by, *76*
    impact on youth confinement
        rates, 87
Rahway State Prison (NJ), 96

*The Relationship between Alcohol,
    Drug Use, and Violence among
    Students* (Community Anti-
    Drug Coalitions of America),
    80
Richey, Warren, 63
Robert Wood Johnson
    Foundation, 8
Roberts, John, 65
Robinson, Laurie O., 95
Rodemeyer, Jamey, 71
Rubin, H. Ted, 58

S
Sandy Hook school shooting
    (CT, 2012), 18–19, 40
Scared straight programs, are
    ineffective, 95–99
Schizophrenia, 25
Schools
    arrests of students for minor
        offenses in, 69–70
    bullying is linked to violence
        in, 33–38
    number of shootings at, 34
    reducing number of guns in,
        39–43
Schwarzenegger, Arnold, 76
Shevlino, April, 46
Shevlino, Peter, 48, 52
Shevlino, Sean, 46–48, 50,
    52–53
Slowikowski, Jeff, 95
Slutkin, Gary, 8, 10
Snyder, Howard, 50
Sotomayor, Sonia, 64
Spengler, William, 21

State(s)
  allowing youth to be
    prosecuted as adults, 70–71
  minimum age provision in,
    59–60
  youth under 18 incarcerated
    in adult prisons by, *51*
Steinberg, Laurence, 48–49
Stolte, Graham, 48
Supreme Court, US, 69, *71*
  bars mandatory life sentences
    for juvenile criminals,
    63–67
  outlaws death penalty for
    offenders under age 18, 52
Surveys
  on link between video-game
    playing and teen violence, *15*
  on marijuana associated with
    crime/delinquent behavior,
    80–82
  of 8th/12th graders, in
    perceived harmfulness of
    marijuana, *81*

T
Taveras, Sara, 89

V
Vera Institute of Justice, 52

Video games/violent video
  games
  contribute to juvenile
    violence, 12–16
  do not contribute to juvenile
    violence, 17–21
  played by children,
    percentage of parents
    monitoring, 19
Virginia Tech shooting (2007),
  35–36

W
Wasserman, Gail, 29
Weapons
  found at Sandy Hook
    Elementary School, *41*
  percentages of students
    threatened/injured with, by
    grade/gender, *42*
  prevalence of student
    carrying, in schools,
    40–41
Webster, Daniel, 7
Wilde, Jessica, 54
Wilson, Scarlett, 50, 52

Y
*Youth Violence and Juvenile
  Justice* (journal), 14

Picture Credits

© Ace Stock Limited/Alamy, 11, 72

© AP Images/Livingston County Daily Press & Argus, Alan Ward, 92

© AP Images/The Post and Courier, Mic Smith, 49

© AP Images/Western Connecticut State University, 20

© Stephen Barnes/Law and Order/Alamy, 98

© Mike Blake/Reuters/Landov, 75

© Bubbles Photolibrary/Alamy, 35

© Connecticut State Police/Getty Images, 41

© LAURENT/DI PASQUALE/BSIP/Alamy, 24

© Norberto Duarte/AFP/Getty Images, 31

© David R. Frazier Photolibrary, Inc./Alamy, 70

© Gale, Cengage, 15, 26, 30, 37, 42, 51, 56, 61, 76, 81, 85, 97

© Spencer Grant/Science Source, 60

© Andrew Lichtenstein/Corbis, 86

© RicoPatuca/Alamy, 44

© Alex Segre/Alamy, 13

© WoodyStock/Alamy, 79